Place is the Passion

Reframing the Israel-Palestine Conflict

Bill Williamson

'Place is the Passion' from a poem by the Palestinian poet,
Mahmoud Darwish signifing homeland for all
who claim the Holy Land as theirs.

"This book is an impressive, yet very readable, survey of the inconvenient complexities of the conflict over Historic Palestine. It exposes the simplicity of the war crimes committed against Palestinians to establish and maintain the State of Israel. And of the all-too-forgotten role that Western powers played and continue to play to the detriment of both Israelis and Palestinians, not to mention peace itself. The book is bold enough to float new thinking while wise enough to note that politics is a living science of the here and now."

Sam Bahour
Writer, activist and prominent American/Palestinian businessman
Ramallah, 2016

"Bill Williamson succeeds in summarising the complexity of Israel/Palestine in a way that demonstrates passionate commitment and intelligent insight. His history of the conflict and the political and social responses from all sides will be valuable to those familiar and new to the issues. The rights based solution to the conflict is set out without idealism or naivety but firmly challenges a status quo that cannot be sustained."

Robert Cohen, Writer and blogger on Jewish affairs
micahsparadigmshift.blogspot.com/

Also by Bill Williamson

From Exam Factories to Communities of Discovery

Beyond Knowledge Management

Lifeworlds and Learning:

Repositioning Higher Education

The Temper of the Times

Class, Culture and Community

Education and Social Change in Egypt and Turkey

Education, Social Structure and Development

First published as a paper back in Great Britain in April 2016
By Comerford and Miller
Under their A Radical Read Imprint
36 Grosvenor Road
West Wickham
BR4 9PY

http://www.radicalread.com
info@radicalread.co.uk

ISBN 978-1-871204-33-9

Printed and Bound in the UK by Dolman Scott, Thatcham Berks

Cover design Howard Lester
Cover image Bill Williamson
Typeset Robbie Griffiths

Contents

Naji Salim al-Ali was a Palestinian cartoonist, noted for the political criticism of the Arab regimes and Israel in his works. He is perhaps best known as creator of the character Handala, pictured in his cartoons as a young witness to the consequences the Palestine Israeli conflict. This cartoon creation has become an icon of Palestinian defiance. On 22 July 1987, while outside the London offices of al-Qabas, a Kuwaiti newspaper for which he drew political caricatures, Naji al-Ali was shot in the face and mortally wounded. He died five weeks later in Charing Cross Hospital. Those responsible for his murder have never been apprehended.

Acknowledgements

The book has its roots in years of personal, political and academic involvement with the Middle East. The people who have worked with me over many years will recognise how much I have built on their support and understanding and the conversations we have had. It is invidious to single them out but I'd like to acknowledge the support and inspiration of Professor Pandelis Glavanis, now of the American University of Cairo, who first introduced me to Palestinians and the troubles of the region they came from about which he is an expert.

Palestinian friends have been for me an invaluable source of insight into the lives of people and their families living under occupation. My understanding of their world has been built up through many hours of conversations covering their family histories, their political and religious outlooks, their hopes and fears. As a sociologist always attuned to how personal worlds are shaped by context and how both change through time, I have listened closely to what they have said about human rights, power, suffering and resistance. I need not mention their names but they know whom I am thinking of.

The descriptors "Palestinian' and 'Jew' quickly break down for me and for members of my family, into faces and stories, to conversations, places, shared meals and friendships. I have written about their world and hope they can recognise the impact their conversations with me have had on how I have come to understand it.

Through meetings with trades unionists, students, civil society groups, political activists in the Palestine Solidarity Campaign I have benefited greatly from having my ideas tested and debated. It is invidious also to single them out but I'd like to acknowledge the support and comradeship of Vin McIntyre who has been a wise and tireless campaigner for human rights in Palestine.

I am particularly indebted to my wife and fellow campaigner, Diane, without whose encouragement and interest this book could not have been written. Our shared interest in the Middle East has been a great open-ended and enjoyable source of strength, friendships and support for us both.

Russell Miller, Editor of the Radical Read series has kept a close watch on me and challenged me to keep my focus and language clear. My failure to meet his high standards is mine alone.

Durham 2016

1

A Land of Milk and Honey?

'a land flowing with milk and honey' – *Exodus* 3:8
'By chance this land became holy' –
Mahmoud Darwish, *Mural*

Memories and identities

In 2017, the world will mark the centenary of the infamous Balfour Declaration. This was the assurance given to Lord Rothschild by the British Foreign Secretary and Christian Zionist, Arthur James Balfour that the British government viewed

> with favour the establishment in Palestine of a National Home for the Jewish people, and will use their best endeavours to facilitate the achievement of this object, it being clearly understood that *nothing shall be done which may prejudice the civil and religious right of existing non-Jewish communities in Palestine, or the rights and political status enjoyed by Jews in any other country.* [1] (My italics)

Lord Rothschild was a leading British Jew able to pass this message to the Zionist leadership then pressing for a Jewish state in Palestine once the war was ended and Ottoman rule destroyed. The Balfour Declaration was for the Zionist movement of Herzl and Weizmann and their supporters in Europe and the USA a major political and diplomatic achievement. In the chaos of war it prised open the possibility of the Jewish state in Palestine they dreamed of.

This moment in the history of Zionism and of what became the state of Israel reminds us today that the tormented history of the Middle East has always been part of the wider international order with its conflicts of interests, deceptions and carefully engineered political alliances that have been and remain to this day in constant flux.

A century later, this declaration is a live symbol in the political memories of both Jews and Arabs. Of course, it is remembered for different reasons. For Jews, it is a turning point opening a new future. For Arabs it is a sign of betrayal, arrogance and hypocrisy on the part of Britain's leaders. The narrative of the memory evokes both the hopes and resentments of two peoples that remain locked in an unresolved conflict about the future of the land then known as Palestine.

The logic behind the declaration was embedded in an imperialist world-view. Britain needed a strong presence in the Middle East to counter French and Russian ambitions in the region and to protect the Suez Canal route to India. There was also a belief among British statesmen that a strong Jewish presence in the Holy Land would accelerate its development and overcome the traditionalism of its Arab population. The exploitation of oil fields in Iraq and the prospects of a future air bridge to India all combined to make a strong case for Jewish settlement in Palestine as something that was in line with imperial interests.

There were immediate pressures at work too. Particularly significant was the need to secure American Jewish support for the US to join the allied war effort and to garner support from European Jews to support imperial aims after the war. [2] Christian Zionist sentiments, based on biblical narratives of the Jewish links with the Holy Land, which were held to be supportive of Jewish settlement in Palestine, was part of the wider worldview of many members of the British government.

The Arab world looked upon this declaration as an act of betrayal of promises that had been given to them that their participation in the allied war effort against the Ottoman Empire would lead to Arab independence. They feared and opposed the prospect of there being a Jewish state in Palestine.

That opposition grew during the inter-war years. It took the form of attacks on Jewish settlements and riots. These troubles fed support for a Palestinian national movement led by the grand mufti of Jerusalem, Hajj Amin al-Husseini. British policies to stem Jewish immigration to Palestine in the years after the war became a source of tension and violence between Mandate authorities and Jewish irregular forces and between Jews and Arabs. The years 1936-39 are of Arab resistance to Jewish settlement and are referred to now as the 'Arab Revolt'.

The Balfour declaration of 1917 opened a door to a new future in Palestine for European Jews. The Hitler regime in Germany was, however, much more decisive in establishing the rationale for a Jewish state. During the pre-war Hitler years Jewish migration to Palestine increased dramatically. After the war and the Holocaust, Jewish migration reached a critical mass that enabled Jews to sustain a political and military struggle to gain their own state. [3]

After world war two, an economically exhausted Britain, harassed by Jewish terrorism in Palestine, was no longer in a position to carry out its Mandate responsibilities. Britain could not resist American pressure to open the gates to Palestine for tens of thousands of Jewish displaced persons in Europe who could not return to their original homelands in Eastern Europe. Mandate responsibilities were transferred to the United Nations. In 1947, the UN agreed to the partition of Palestine in a deal that was very generous to Jews and which Arabs regarded as an unjust settlement that they resisted.

Palestinian Loss of Land 1947–Present

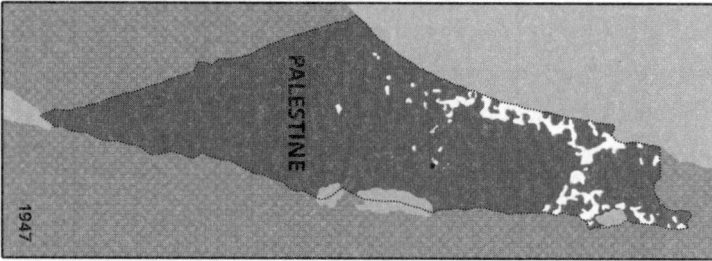

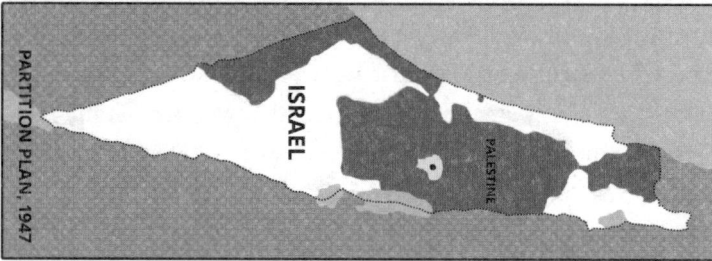

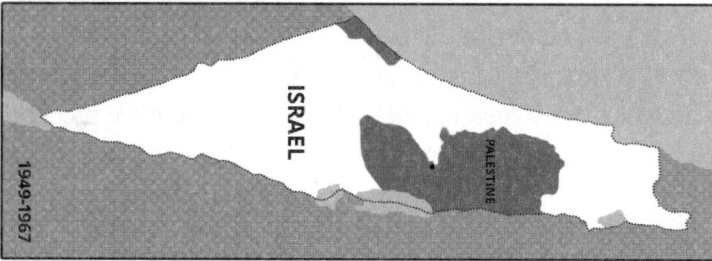

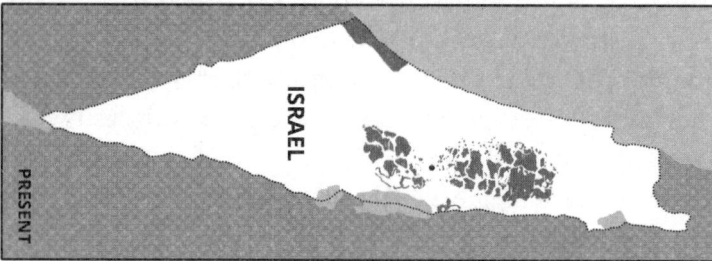

In May 1948, after months of struggle between Arabs and Jews in the Holy Land and of international efforts to try and delay the partition plan, David Ben Gurion, of the Provisional State Council and Jewish Agency, declared independence for the state of Israel. The state that came into being fulfilled a Zionist dream. It was not the outcome that the British envisaged in 1917 or even in 1947. Without strong American support and arm-bending diplomacy behind the scenes in the UN, it would not have been possible at all.

Nor was it clear, even among Zionists, what the future of Palestine and Israel would be. The American Council for Judaism for instance took an anti-Zionist position and favoured a state that would be democratic and secular and one in which Jews and Arabs would have equal rights. [4] This, of course, was not the Zionist plan. Nor were the Arab states of the region prepared to accept the partition of Palestine.

The logics of change

The Balfour Declaration was a product of a moment of conflict and change in an imperialist world order. It was during that moment that a well-organized Zionist movement used all political means open to it to influence the decisions of leaders in the world's most powerful nation states. There was no historical necessity at work in this, no predetermined outcome, only a penetrating analysis of a situation, a clear articulation of goals and purposeful action. Viewed this way, the Balfour Declaration was not a gift; it was a political achievement.

The emergence of the state of Israel after the Second World War was also not inevitable. It was a product of circumstances: Hitler's war against the Jews; the growth of American power and western fears over the rise of Arab nationalism and, after 1950, of Russian influence in the Middle East. Each generated constraints and opportunities that limited and shaped the possibilities open to the main political actors in the region.

Through a combination of British weakness, American support, the incompetence of the Arab leadership and determined, ruthless action by well-led Jewish forces, Israel pulled successfully through what the country now celebrates as its 'war of independence'. It is an event Palestinians remember as the *Nakba*, or catastrophe.

Facets of the history of the Israel-Palestine conflict since this period will be discussed throughout this book. It is part of a framework of strategic alliances, national interests, foreign policies and political identities that is in a continuous state of development and flux. Because of this, the future of this conflict cannot be predicted or determined. It will be decided through political and possibly military action.

The matter will not be through bi-lateral negotiations or the military success of one party over the other. For politicians who parrot this line, it is a shameful cop-out. The Jewish settlements built on Palestinian land have been denounced by the UN as illegal. This is an issue that needs to be rectified not negotiated. To do otherwise is like asking a family who have been victims of an armed-robbery to negotiate with the thieves how much of their property should be returned with the added imposition that the criminals can carry their weapons to the negotiating table. Real negotiations presuppose equal partners to the process and for Palestinians at the moment there is no prospect of these conditions being achieved.

If the future for Israelis and Palestinians is to be a peaceful one, it must come from profound changes in the structures of Middle Eastern politics and of western approaches to this region. Western politicians and diplomats who parrot the line that there can be no settlement of this conflict without bi-lateral agreements between Israelis and Palestinians over the key issues of boundaries, settlements, Jerusalem and refugees, are prevaricating. They are bogged down in a pro-Israeli stance that leaves them in a state of denial about the kind of state their policies support. They are unwilling to take the action needed to change the political circumstances to enable proper, balanced negotiations could take place.

The challenge for those who seek a peaceful Middle East and a political resolution of the Israel-Palestine conflict is to find ways to exert pressure on western states to compel changes in their policies towards this region. Current approaches support Israel in policies towards Palestinians that are oppressive, racist and violent. They have encouraged the growth in Israel of political forces that are wholly opposed to the Palestinian right of self-determination. They have created a state whose actions have undermined any prospect of a peace settlement based on the idea of two states living side by side. Confident in their military superiority and sure of American support, Israeli leaders have been determined to shape the future of the state independently of the needs and aspirations of millions of Palestinians living in Israel, in besieged Gaza and the occupied territories (OTs) of the West Bank.

The image that Israel presents to the world as the West's 'democratic ally in the Middle East' has worn very thin. Israel is now dominated by a right wing, religious political bloc intolerant of democratic politics. It has grown in importance and power over the past quarter century in line with the growth of illegal Jewish settlements on the West bank. In 2015, Israel remembered the 20th anniversary of the assassination by a right-wing orthodox Jew of Prime Minister Rabin, one of the architects of the Oslo Accords that created the Palestinian Authority and endorsed the idea of a future peace deal based on two states living securely. To the likes of Yigal Amir, the assassin, Rabin was a traitor. Right wing groups in Israel still regard him as a hero and have campaigned for his release from prison. His murder of the Prime Minister can in retrospect be seen as the beginning of the end of the peace process.

The secular, democratic and socialist state Israel's western supporters thought was being built after the war that would 'make the desert bloom' is a nostalgic fiction. Until western leaders realise this and seek to neutralise the power of right wing pro-Israeli lobbies in Congress, in the EU and in their national parliaments, there is no prospect of a peace deal in Palestine.

This is not a council of despair. Israel is not yet a totalitarian state impervious to both external pressure and political opposition from within. Nor are Palestinians by some natural flaw implacable anti-Semites opposed to Israel and unwilling to make peace. Palestinians have opposed the occupation of their land and the territorial expansion of Israel and suffered greatly as a result. The forms their opposition has taken have been shaped by the logic of Israel power. Faced with a military Leviathan, armed resistance has been futile.

Civil disobedience has been their weapon of choice. As the Israeli occupation intensified following the 1967 'Six Day War' armed resistance became an option and since the mid 1980s that took the form of suicide bombing and rocket attacks. At the edges of Palestinian resistance, some groups found strength and political rationale in Islam. This enables them so see the plight of Palestinians under Israeli rule as a symbol of western oppression of Muslims across the world.

In the climate of the contemporary Middle East, this could be construed as a dangerous development, not just for Israel and the West but also for Palestinian political development. When religious fanaticism drives politics, politics as the peaceful resolution of conflicts fails. Such developments have, nevertheless resulted from Israeli actions, especially its relentless siege and destructive wars on Gaza over the past decade.

Whatever might be said about the rights and wrongs of this interpretation of events, one thing is clear: great changes have and are taking place in both Israel and Palestine and in the international order of which they are a part. Hope lies in the possibility of guiding these changes in the direction of peace. To do that, we have to probe as deeply as we can into the social and political dynamics of both Israel and Palestine to understand why both societies are as they are and why their leaders make the choices they do.

Structures and actions

The Balfour Declaration was a product of the age of empires. The conflicts which followed it after the First World War, a period which Eric Hobsbawm the historian, characterised as the 'age of catastrophe' were driven by the clashing interests of nation states and of two competing ideological systems: capitalism and communism. [5] They united for a while at great cost to defeat Fascism. By the late 1940s, powerful Empires had crumbled and a new age of superpowers had begun creating transnational structures of governance and political alliance that shaped a new world order. Israel built a place for itself within that order, consolidating its military superiority as a western ally that cultivated American support and exploited Arab weaknesses.

Four interdependent but different social structures need to be understood to explore thoroughly the political dynamics of this situation and find better ways forward to a peaceful region. They are: 'Israel', 'Palestine' 'the Arab world' and 'the West'. Their names are in inverted commas because, as the book shows, each is a social and political construct. Unlike other countries and nation states, these have no clear geographical boundaries or settled national identities. They are political fictions, products of entwined hopes, economic alliances and powerful interests.

'The West' is shorthand for a complex, transnational network of strategic alliances, economic relationships binding together some of the world's powerful nation states and their corporate and military elites. It is a network beyond the reach of the democratic controls of its member nations whose citizens poorly understand its mechanisms for decision-making. Indeed, without access to the kind of information now exposed by the release of secret diplomatic messages and National Security Agency reports by the CIA administrator, Edward Snowden, elected representatives in western parliaments would not properly understand the deals, the political machinations, the surveillance and the violence – including the use of torture – that make it possible for the global behemoth of the 'West' to function as it does. There is a normally hidden and dangerous world behind the political platitudes deployed to justify foreign policies.

Western influence in the Middle East and in the politics of the Israel-Palestine conflict has been decisive in shaping its course and consequences. Without western support, Israel could not have developed to become the state it is today. Without western financial support through aid programmes the political institutions of Palestinian life would have collapsed long ago.

'The Arab world' is a complex construct of nation states that have much in common – particularly the shared religion of Islam – but much to differentiate them. Arab hostility to Israel, at least until 1973, has been the key factor in ensuring that Israel, with western support, built up its formidable defence forces to become the dominant military power in the region. In retrospect, it seems paradoxical that during the late 1950s and 1960s Israel built working political and military relationships with Iran and Turkey, but especially Iran. This policy, known by Israeli politicians as 'the alliance with the periphery' was developed to build relationships that were useful to both Iran and Israel in the containment of Arab nationalism.

This changed, of course, with the overthrow of the Shah in 1979. After the Khomeini revolution, Israel became the 'Zionist entity' to which the revolutionary Shia regime was opposed. Through

Hezbollah, formed after Israel's 1986 invasion of Lebanon, Iran has helped sustain a northern threat to Israel. Iran's nuclear energy programme became for Israel leaders something they understood as an existential threat to their state. They campaigned hard internationally to forestall agreements between the West – especially the USA – and Iran about an inspection regime of Iran's nuclear plants that would prevent the development of nuclear weapons that could be aimed at Israel.

'Israel 'and 'Palestine' are imagined states in the sense that those who identify with them and feel a strong sense of belonging and obligation to them feel that their countries are not yet fully formed. Right-wing politicians and movements in Israel see their country as trapped in artificial historical boundaries and they are determined to expand beyond them. The historic mission of Zionism is to reclaim *Eretz Israel* (the land of Israel) as the state and homeland of Jews.

Palestinians cleave to the hope that one day they will reclaim land currently occupied by Israel and secure their rights to return to homes they were driven from by Jewish forces from 1947 onwards. For the past two decades, Palestinian political leaders, with western and Arab support, have worked towards a resolution of the conflict that will bring into being a Palestinian state with Jerusalem as its capital that will live in peace and security alongside Israel.

Futures Uncertain

The two-state solution is a political dream that has faded. Palestinians are divided among themselves about what a Palestinian state should look like. Israel's leaders have shown no willingness to agree to any peace deal that will result in defined borders. Further conflict looks inevitable. Despite that, there is a fresh approach out of the current political impasse. It builds that case on four main ideas.

The first is that it there can be no precisely agreed deal that would settle it. The best that can be achieved *at this time* is to work to build the conditions for dialogue that stand a chance of discovering a new way forward to peace.

At the moment, the future for Palestine is decided by Israel and is essentially closed. It has to be prised free of the Israeli grip for new possibilities within it to be realised.

Secondly, a peaceful resolution of this conflict necessarily involve social and political changes not only in Israel and the occupied and besieged territories of Palestine but also in the societies of the West and the Arab world. The key task is to engage citizens critically and democratically with the political life of their countries to build foreign policies and alliances conducive to peace. It is particularly important to press international institutions such as the European Union and the United Nations to change the field of forces and policies that maintain the current status quo.

Thirdly, that the descriptors 'Israelis' and 'Palestinians' cannot refer to fixed national or cultural identities and stereotypical images of the two peoples condemned to conflict. Each has become what the conflict has made them and both have changed over time. Because of this, there is hope for the future. In the future, 'Israel' and 'Palestine' can be very different to what they are now.

The fourth idea is that the changes required will be hard won and are needed urgently. They demand a refocusing of public debate about foreign policies onto human rights. The new approach is based on hope rather than fear and the careful political isolation of fanatics. It demands calibrated actions to make Israel pay the costs of its occupation and the destruction caused by its actions. It involves exposing the political deficiencies and ideological hypocrisies of western policies towards the whole Middle East.

Fortunately, there is much to build on and there are people of goodwill on both sides of this conflict who seek a just, mutually beneficial and sustainable solution to it that protects the human rights of all. If the 'West' can play a stronger role in releasing both Israelis and Palestinians from the dreadful constraints of occupation, there is no doubt they will find a better way forward to live together.

In a prescient essay he wrote in 1935 on the difficulties writers had to write truthfully under Fascism, the German poet and playwright Bertolt Brecht argued that it was vital to expose the avoidable causes of the barbarism people suffered from. [6] His point was that when the causes were known, they could be opposed. This book invites debate about the barbarism causing the suffering of both Israelis and Palestinians locked as they are in a structure of relationships and power that meets the long-term interests of neither.

Given the amplifying dangers of the conflicts of the Middle East and the failure of the inaptly named and sclerotic peace process in the Israel-Palestine conflict, the call here to debate it in a focused way is not an empty gesture. In the absence of what the sociologist, Karl Mannheim, a Hungarian Jewish academic driven out of Germany in the 1930s and a prescient critic of totalitarianism in the 1940s called a 'diagnosis of our time' – and we do lack such a diagnosis – the most important political step that can be taken is to develop one and to open up the road to a better future.

Israeli politicians like to claim to international audiences that peace will only be discovered through unconditional negotiations between Israelis and Palestinians. They add that Israel has no negotiating partner since Palestinians will not recognize the Jewish state of Israel. Until there is a balance of power in the negotiation processes there can be no agreements. Israeli power is inseparable from that of the USA and of its European allies. The policies, strategic alliances, economic ties and carefully cultivated political sympathies that connect them form a matrix of power that makes the continuing oppression of Palestinians possible. It ensures, too, their resistance. Peace will come when this matrix of power is loosened and new options for the future become imaginable. This requires a massive shift in public opinion and sustained efforts to loosen the political grip of the ideological fanatics on the Holy Land and across the Middle East.

2

The Constant Conflict

The Israel-Palestine conflict has been a problem of global significance for more than sixty years. All attempts to find a credible framework for peace have failed. The 'two-state solution' that has guided these is now widely acknowledged to be moribund and there is nothing to take its place. On present trends, the future will not be one of peaceful collaboration between two secure, independent states but of a vilified, pariah, Israeli-dominated apartheid state that blights the security, hopes and human rights of those it oppresses. The tragedy of it is that the world looks on powerless to prevent it.

There are, however, options available that respect the human rights and protect the security of both Israelis and Palestinians and which secure the social, economic and cultural development of the region as a whole. To discover and realise them, there needs to be a radical rethinking among western and Arab leaders of their policies towards Israel. Step one towards such a goal is to be clearer about the historical and political context of the conflict and the daily news of violence it generates. It is to build a critical distance between western audiences and the way Israel and its supporters abroad and the predominantly pro-Israeli western media routinely portray its actions.

A *history of violence*

Throughout its entire existence and territorial expansion since 1948, the Israeli state has been on a war footing. Following a short period of relative peace after the battles of 1948/9 during what Israel calls its 'war if independence', there was in 1956, in collusion with France and Britain, an Israel attack on Egypt. In the 'Six-Day War" of 1967, Israel was at war with the attacking forces of Egypt, Jordan and Syria. Throughout the 1970s, Israel was at war against the Palestine Liberation Organisation (PLO) in Lebanon. Egyptian forces attacked and were defeated by Israel in the 1973 Yom Kippur war. In 1982 there was a full scale Israeli invasion of southern Lebanon that ended in one of the darkest chapters of Israeli military history: the Shatila and Sabra refugee camp massacre in 1982. In 2006, Israel invaded Lebanon once more with massive destruction and loss of life. Open military conflict has happened in Gaza on three occasions: in 2009, 2012 and 2014.

The prevalent Israeli interpretation of this history is the defensive one i.e. that Israel has been compelled to engage in military operations against Arab armies and Palestinian terrorists in order to defend the security of its citizens and the state. The contrary view is that the long-term, underlying, determined, oppressive expansion of Israel is the essence of it founding ideology: Zionism.

Either by choice or ignorance, successive western leaders have failed properly to recognise that the Israeli drive for statehood and its actions in respect of the Palestinians has throughout its sixty-year history been a project of colonisation and population displacement.

The relentless logic of conflict and war has its parallel in the regular failures in peace negotiations. These have been going on since 1948. They have taken the form of truce and armistice arrangements, bi-lateral agreements between Israel and Arab states such as Jordan and Egypt – especially the Camp David talks that led to the Israel-Egypt peace treaty in 1978 – and internationally sponsored peace talks and framework agreements such as the Oslo Accord of 1993 that set up the Palestinian Authority. Since then, there have been many rounds of negotiations, often with external help from the Arab League or the United States, to manage ceasefires or agree prisoner exchanges, but none that dealt with the underlying drivers of the conflict.

From secular Zionism to the 'Jewish State'

Israel has sought legitimacy in the eyes of the world in different ways at different times. In the nineteenth century, the Zionist project to build a Jewish homeland in the Holy Land was justified on ethno-nationalist grounds. Jews, it was claimed, like any other nation, had a right to a homeland of their own. This Zionist vision was not widely shared among Jews. Among assimilated Jews in Europe, there were fears that Zionism would create anti-Semitism and reinforce ideas about Jews not really being part of the societies they lived in.

Nevertheless, Zionists became successful in both Europe and in the United States in persuading western leaders of their case. During the years before World War One, under the threat of pogroms in Eastern Europe and Russia and in the inter-war years of the twentieth century, Jewish migration to Western Europe and the United Sates and also to Palestine increased. After the Second World War, Israel became the safe haven for Jews who had suffered the Nazi genocide. At this time, Israel presented to the world as a secular, socialist project that would re-fashion the Middle East.

In this guise, despite the atrocities committed by Jewish irregular forces against Palestinians and British Mandate forces from 1945 to 1948, it has had the support of many western political leaders and often most enthusiastically from those on the left. In the UK Labour Party, even left-wingers like Aneuran Bevan and Michael Foot were ardent supporters of the young state. They knew the leaders of the Israeli Labour Party and saw in their policies a socialist project that would modernise and change a reactionary Middle East. [1] In Germany, through a mixture of shame and guilt, but also from the need detected by Konrad Adenauer, post-war Germany's Chancellor, to build a strong alliance with the United States, political support for Israel was strong and has remained so.

The 1967 war and the occupation of the West Bank, the Golan Heights and Gaza was seen by Israeli leaders as the recovery of the biblical lands of Judea and Samaria for the Jewish people. The Israeli historian, Shlomo Sand, says of this 'linguistic engineering' that it 'enabled Jewish nationalist memory to make its astonishing leap back in time over the territory's long non-Jewish history.' [2]

These events rekindled a theological justification for the Israeli state and its actions. Fanatical religious Zionists, against the opposition of some Israeli political and military leaders, expressed clear hopes that Jerusalem would no longer be a divided city and that its Muslim sites, the Dome of the Rock in particular, one of Islam's holiest sites, should be destroyed. [3] As it gathered political momentum, this posture strengthened support for the growth of illegal West Bank Jewish settlements that rendered any two-state solution to the conflict with the Palestinians impossible. At the same time, the growth of settlements shifted Israeli politics decisively to the right.

The colonizing project has been maintained through every failed negotiation and has been widely acknowledged to be the major obstacle to peace in the region. There have been Israeli leaders such as Prime Minister Olmert, (in office from 2006 to 2009) who were prepared to evacuate the West Bank settlements but the settler movement developed a political momentum of its own, driven hard by a religious ideological fervour that was immune to rational political dialogue. Under Prime Minister Benjamin Netanyahu, right-wing calls for Israel to consolidate its identity as a *'Jewish state'* increased. This was a far cry from the founding ideology of the state as a secular, democratic one respecting the rights of all its citizens.

Expansion and resistance

Building the state of Israel is a project that over half a century bred the resistance from Palestinians. Palestinians became for many Israelis the dangerous 'other' with whom it was impossible to negotiate. The Israel occupation of lands seized in 1967 became a military fait accompli, a prize to be retained and one that the defeated powers of the Arab world, including Palestinians, had little choice but to accept. This is the doctrine that might is right; that the victors in a battle have the right to impose their will on the defeated.

Of course, no Palestinian, especially those 700,000 people displaced from their homeland in 1948 and the tens of thousands moved on again in 1967 could ever accept that. They felt justified by the terms of international law governing the behaviour of occupying powers i.e. that it is illegal to settle areas with victorious combatants, to resist the Israeli occupation and to continue to demand within international law the right of return of refugees. In this they have had the support of the international community through the agency of the United Nations and its many resolutions on this conflict.

Seen from these points of view, the conflict is beyond solution. Israel, as the strongest player on the field with the best equipped army in the region, a force backed up by US military aid and with the ultimate threat to use the nuclear weapons it has never acknowledged possessing, has been under no compulsion to accept the premises of the United Nations about the illegality of its occupation.

Nor has Israel needed to fear the threat of military action from Palestinians or their ostensible Arab supporters. The asymmetry in power and influence has ensured that Israel could with impunity dictate the terms of any political negotiations with Palestinians to its own advantage. Through its US-supported military power and political determination, Israel gained control of Palestine.

Across the Arab world, this conflict has become a lightning conductor that diverts energy and anger towards Israel and the West and offers pro-western Arab leaders the chance to express a solidarity with Palestinians that plays well with Arab public opinion without carrying any obligation to act in their support. Since the 1967 war, the Arab states have lived with the knowledge that even if they wanted to they have not had the ability to challenge Israel militarily in support of the liberation of Palestine. Indeed, some Arab leaders, especially in Lebanon and Jordan, saw the Palestine Liberation Organisation (PLO) and thousands of Palestinian refugees as a political and ideological threat to their own societies.

Palestinians have been living in a permanent state of what the British writer and art critic John Berger, a regular visitor to Palestine, has called, 'undefeated despair', a stance, he says, that is without fear, without resignation, without a sense of defeat. [4] It sustains their constant resistance to an occupation that is imposed by a stranglehold that is economic, geographical, civic and military. Despite this, he claims, Israel has not crushed their spirit and their hopes.

Palestinian resistance to the occupation has been continuous and has taken many different forms. It is the central political dynamic of Palestinian life and is as unstoppable as the Zionist drive forward that it opposes. The Palestinian struggle against the Israeli occupation seized the headlines of international news in the late 1960s with the hijacking of the Rome to Athens flight by the Leila Khaled, a member of the Popular Front for the Liberation of Palestine. At the Munich Olympics of 1972 a group of Palestinians from the Black September Movement murdered two Israeli Olympic athletes. In the shoot out that followed, eleven Israelis died along with five Palestinians and a German police officer.

These were shocking attacks and across the world Palestine became inextricably associated with international terror. Resistance to Israel continued in many other ways. It is was expressed through street demonstrations, mass movements of protest – such as the *Intifadas* (uprisings) of 1987 and 2001 – and it has taken the violent forms of suicide bombing and terror attacks. In Gaza and in Lebanon it took an overt military character with rocket attacks on Israel and street fighting with Israeli forces.

Armed struggle was the dominant theme of Palestinian resistance in the years preceding the Oslo Accords and its rationale was less the military overthrow of Israel than a means to establish a Palestinian political identity for the world to see. [5] Resistance also became a central theme of Palestinian literature and cultural life. Through theatre, film, poetry and literature culture has become, as the great figure of Palestinian letters, Edward Said has said, is 'a way of fighting against extinction and obliteration'. It is 'is a form of memory against effacement'. [6]

Palestinians have paid a high price for their resistance – in lost lives, imprisonment and routine humiliation and economic deprivation, but they have been willing to pay it. Resistance restored self-respect and dignity in circumstances that have been designed to destroy both. Those who have died through resistance are celebrated as martyrs.

Most Israelis, despite being citizens of the most well-armed state in the Middle East, lead lives framed by the constant and as they see it, amplifying threat of terror from Arab and Iranian neighbours. The tragedy of the situation is that no one is content with it and few see a way out of it. Given the history of peace negotiations, the pessimists are right. There is no solution. We need, therefore, a different view both of what peace might mean and of how it can be achieved.

The newspeak of peace

The 'peace process' as it is has so far been understood, became a cover for the expansion of illegal Israeli settlements on the West Bank and for the continued siege of Gaza. Israel's territorial expansion has made the prospect of a viable Palestinian state unrealisable. Some critics characterised the consequences for Palestinian political life as *politicide*. [7] Baruch Kummerling, the Israeli sociologist who coined the term, saw it as a process of destroying the possibility of an independent political life for Palestinians. As an objective of Israeli policy it accelerated after 1967 and particularly under the leadership of Prime Minister Ariel Sharon.

The consequences of the 'peace process' became wholly counter-productive. They have resulted in the alienation of many ordinary Palestinians from politics. The position of political Islamists in Palestine, especially in Gaza has been strengthened. The failure of talks strengthened the destructive potential of the Israeli right-wing and the settler movement, the groups in Israeli society violently opposed to any agreement with the Palestinians.

Those in the United States and in Europe who support Israel and defend it actions do so with a passionate fervour and ruthless effectiveness. They are well organised in powerful lobbies like the American Israeli Public Affairs Committee (AIPAC) or the

Parliamentary Friends of Israel groups in all the main parties in the House of Commons in the UK and in the European Parliament. These lobbies are well organised to fend off criticism of Israeli policies and actions and are active in maintaining the narrative that the state they support is the perpetual victim whose military operations are always legitimately defensive ones.

Such support is a useful cover for the continuing trade in arms that is a key part of the relationship between Israel and other nation states. America and Israel's armament industries are closely related. Germany has a special relationship with Israel in the market for arms. To take just one example: over the past decade Germany has supplied five Dolphin class submarines to Israel that are capable of carrying nuclear weapons and of policing the coastline of Iran. The Israeli defence Minister Ehud Barak told reporters from the magazine *Der Spiegel*, "Germany can be proud of the fact that they have secured the existence of the State of Israel for many years to come." [8]

Building critical distance

Arms trading and intelligence sharing with Israel, including weapons development research and military R&D, as well as academic collaboration through European Union programmes such as the Horizon Program and trading agreements with the European Union (EU), have been the ties that bind Israel to the West. They are the scaffold to give material support to the ideological claims about Israel as a 'democratic ally' or a 'Jewish homeland' that is under constant threat of 'terror'. Such claims neutralise western criticism of Israel while strengthening mutual support.

In the 2014 Israeli attack on Gaza, for example, nearly all western leaders who urged ceasefires and peace talks between the combatants, prefaced their comments on the Israeli action, which was condemned by many as disproportionate to the point of being criminal, with the formulaic response that: 'Israel has a right to defend itself against rocket attacks and to live in peace'. They did not say the same about Palestinians in Gaza who for a decade have been subjected to siege conditions, to drone attacks, bombing runs by F-16 jets, targeted assassinations and ground troop incursions.

And here stands the so far unmet challenge for the future: how can a new narrative be built that looks beyond the current logic of the situation in this conflict and which is based around human rights and justice for Palestinians? The same point applies to Israeli society and its people. What has been done to Palestinians in their name is by any standard of justice and rational international politics, simply wrong, both legally and morally. Such policies have corroded the moral character of Israeli society as much as they have inflicted pain and humiliation on Palestinians. In doing so, they have added to the political instability of the Middle East and the wider international community.

Interlocked identities

Given that 'Israel' and 'Palestine' are imagined communities that are tied together historically with political and personal identities that have developed in mutual, though often violent interaction, it is clear that the peaceful resolution of their conflict has to involve profound social changes in both.

Each society involved in this conflict has over time defined the character of the other. The decades-long struggle between them has shaped their social structures, their institutions, their cultures and modes of thinking, their attitudes and values. These features of each society do reflect some essential quality that is either Jewish-Israeli or Palestinian, but have emerged in the context of patterns of migration to Israel, in years of conflict and in the political failure to find new solutions to it.

Both societies are changing, and in very different ways. Israel is a sociological enigma: a modern society in the modern world breaking all the rules of modernity. The work of Zygmunt Bauman, the Polish (and secular Jewish) sociologist, theorist of modernity and author of one of the most important studies of the Holocaust ever written,[9] is dominated by the theme of what he calls 'liquid modernity'.[10] Modern societies he says are open to the world. Attitudes and identities have become detached from place and nation. Utopias, he argues, are no longer fixated on building paradise in particular places. The happiness people seek in the world of the future is no longer tied to a cause or a place but has become personal, bound to social relationships that, on account of new technologies of communication, can be global.

Even if we concede there is some hyperbole in Bauman's descriptions of our interdependent, *globalised* world order, modern Israel stands out as an exception. Here, for a growing and politically significant section of society, the desired future is in the past; the highest hopes and aspirations of its people have become focused on a particular place – *Eretz Israel* – with undefined geographical boundaries. The Palestinian poet, Mahmoud Darwish's line that 'Place is the Passion' is an apt characterisation of the powerful, ostensibly Jewish sentiment, gripping the throat of Israeli politics.

Far from being open to the world, Israel is becoming a closed community, a place for Jews alone. With its separation barrier snaking around the West Bank, the country is to some Israelis taking on the character of a *shtetl*. The paradox is that as the religious right-wing of Israeli politics has gained in strength, the *Jewish* character of the society is increasingly debated and problematical. Secular Jews are as varied in their outlooks as any group of people and increasingly critical of the growing numbers of orthodox Jews who eschew the modern world.

These cultural differences among Israelis raise big questions: what does it mean to be Jewish in Israel? What could the idea of a *Jewish state*, which is what the Israeli leaders expect Palestinians and the world to recognise, possibly mean? Can secular Jews be part of it? If so, then such an idea can have no religious foundation. If religion is not the qualification of membership, then it must be ethnicity and such a state cannot be a state for all its citizens. In which case a Jewish state would become inevitable, as many have claimed, an apartheid state, vilified by the world community.

Palestine, on the other hand, is a society with only a future to look forward to but without an agreed political or cultural order from within which to articulate what shape that future should have and, at the moment, no power to direct it. With the Israeli jackboot on its neck, Palestine has no option other than to resist the imposed reality of its oppressor.

Reframing the problem

The key task now is radical and fourfold: it is to nurture through debate a greater *understanding* across the world about the roots and catalysts of the Israel-Palestine conflict. Without that, the citizens of western societies will continue as in the past either to be indifferent towards what is being done in their name in the Middle East or swamped by the complexity of the region's problems and the distortions of its propaganda. Secondly, it is to *expose* and *challenge* the core beliefs, language and assumptions that lie behind the propaganda surrounding all aspects of the conflict. Thirdly, since changes in attitudes and perceptions do not occur without both external stimulus and pressure and since powerful interests frame the debate about this conflict, those who support peaceful solutions based on human rights, have to *campaign* hard for change. Finally, all campaigning would be useless if there was not view of a better future to ignite the imagination and to encourage people to *discover* pathways towards it.

Linda Grant, the acclaimed British, Jewish novelist spent months in Israel and wrote when she returned:

> I left Israel, on 31st January 2004, burdened by a sense of horror, for a thought had occurred to me that was unbearable: that at its heart, indeed because of what is in the hearts of its people, not just its leaders, this conflict might be insoluble. [11]

Five years later, in 2011 the British journalist and writer, Jonathan Freedland who is also Jewish and who knows Israel well, commented on a role-playing seminar he had attended about the Israel-Palestine conflict. The Israelis in this seminar who played the roles of Palestinians argued vehemently for a state of their own. They demanded the right of return of refugees and for Jerusalem to be the capital of the Palestinian state they hoped for. Similarly, Palestinians playing Israeli roles expressed deep anxieties about security and suspicion about the integrity of the leaders of Arab states and Palestinians when they said they would acknowledge Israel's right to exist.

Both groups quickly became locked into their different negotiating positions. Neither party could look beyond them to imagine the outlines of a peace deal. Freedland summed it up:

> Those apart from this conflict who claim to care about one or both peoples should take note. There is no shortage of friends of the Israelis or advocates of the Palestinians. What's missing are friends of peace itself. [12]

The view taken here is that there is a peace to be discovered and to find it much more open, critical debate is needed about the futures of Israel and of Palestine in the context of the wider Middle East.

Until those who drive this conflict from their bases in foreign policy establishments, armaments companies, faith communities and political parties are questioned about the long-term consequences of their decisions and their support for particular leaders and states, the Middle East will remain mired in violence and on the knife-edge of a regional and perhaps global war.

Radical pragmatism

These four tasks listed above – understanding, challenging, campaigning and discovering – are linked. Together they provide the basis for a critical dialogue that will generate new ideas and perspectives on what seem at the moment intractable problems. Work on these tasks can be carried out at different levels and across the world but especially in countries and organisations that are deeply implicated in the decision-making that is shaping the politics of the Middle East.

Social and political change is needed not only within Israeli and Palestinian societies but also in the western societies that are so deeply implicated in the Middle East. For example, Tony Judt, the British, Jewish historian who spent many years in American academic life, noted of American Jews that they were assimilated into American society; that they speak neither Yiddish nor Hebrew; that they lacked a deep knowledge of Jewish religious traditions and unlike the Poles or the Irish have no direct memories of 'the old country'. [13]

What binds American Jews together, he claims, is Auschwitz and support for Israel. Their concern for both developed long after the war, particularly after the Six Day War of 1967. By then, it had become possible to discuss the Holocaust openly and an American interest in human rights was easily transferred as support for and identification with Israel, a society portraying itself as being permanently on the brink of another genocide.

Judt explained his view as follows:

> Auschwitz stands for the past: the memory of the
> suffering of other Jews in other places at other times.
> Israel represents the present: Jewish achievement in the
> form of an aggressive, self-confident military state – the
> anti-Auschwitz.

Such an identification has a powerful emotional resonance and
his interlocutor in this book, another Jewish academic historian,
Timothy Snyder, added a further telling gloss on Judt's argument.
He said American Jews did not identify with Israel as such but
with the Likud, with the Israeli right, a group, he says that 'makes
its American audience feel bad – and they, in turn, authorize it to
behave badly'. The result, for both historians is that the Jewish-
American identification with Israel is a 'perverse and unhealthy'
notion of Jewishness.

There are other groups in American society for whom Israel
has a strong emotional resonance, though for different reasons
to those that explain Jewish-American support. In post 9/11
America, for example, pride in American values, fear of terrorism
and suspicions about Islam have for many fused together into
anger and support to be tough in 'the war on terror'. It is a feeling
that inclines Americans, especially among the Christian right, to
be strongly pro-Israel.

Nevertheless, pro-Palestinian campaigns across Europe and
elsewhere in the world have strengthened. Israel is no longer seen
as the David defending itself against the Arab Goliath. Zionist
claims to an ancient territorial, moral and genetic bond to the
land of Israel, are increasingly debated both for their historical
accuracy and contemporary political relevance. The once
dominant Israeli narrative is unravelling, though not quickly
enough among western political leaders.

3
Breaking the power of the past

New thinking about the Israel-Palestine conflict starts with scepticism about how its central protagonists and their supporters abroad interpret its history. Israel's proudly remembered 'war of independence' is the sadly recalled Palestinian *Nakba* or catastrophe. The one gave the Jews of Palestine and across the world a profound sense of hope and liberation; the other left Palestinians with a profound sense of loss of their land and heritage.

Living the past

The people of Israel and Palestine live within the past as if in an iron cage. It is inescapable. Its legacies frame every conversation about politics. They are written into the landscape, it settlements patterns, its road systems and its water supplies. Above all, it is written into the memories and anxieties of Israelis and Palestinians.

Two small but telling examples of this: during a visit to Israel in 2012 my wife and I fell into conversation with an armed Israeli tourist policeman in Jerusalem at the Haas promenade, a beauty spot with views over the Old City. He was keen to practise his English and to be friendly towards visitors. It turned out he was from Austria; that his parents had survived incarceration in the Theresienstadt concentration camp and that he came to Israel after the war as a German-speaking child. Knowing no Hebrew, he was teased by his Israeli compatriots for being a 'Nazi' so he learned to fight back. He became a soldier and eventually fought as a paratrooper in the 1967 war.

We talked about many things and at one point I asked him: 'What does it mean to you to be Jewish?' He said: 'I'm Jewish because my mother was Jewish!' 'What about God and the Torah and the faith?' I asked. 'Look', he said, 'I'm not religious. The Jews have their God, the Christians have their God, the Muslims have their God. I don't care about that. They can have their Gods. I'm an Israeli!'

Just at that point, a family of orthodox Jews walked by. I pointed to them and said: 'What about people like that? What do you think of them?' He said: 'Do you want me to be honest?' I said; 'Of course!' He said: 'To tell you the truth, I hate them! They don't serve in the army. They did nothing to defend Israel in 1967 and they demand to be looked after.' Then, with chilling anger, he said: 'If I could, I would kill them!'

The second conversation: after visiting the West Bank and feeling both astonished and shocked at the extent of settlement building and the absurd brutality of the separation barrier snaking its ugly way across the landscape and the constant presence of Israeli checkpoints, I mentioned to an Israeli friend and writer that Israel's presence on the West Bank resembled the apparatus of a fascist state.

'What you must understand' she said 'is that today, in Israel, it is 1933'. She quickly added: 'No one is planning the genocide of Palestinians' but, she explained, 'religious obscurantism has seeped into the Jewish psyche and settler power dictates everything'. She felt strongly that the colonisation of the once wholly secular Israeli state by religion actually alienates Jewish people from their real heritage. It has allowed them 'to throw off the burden of compassion', to wallow in a sense of permanent victimhood and to embrace what she called 'a paradigm of righteous illegality'.

The only reason she had left to continue living in Israel was to oppose it.

She was full of foreboding for the future. She said that the Israel she knew is now courting destruction on several fronts. She objected strongly to the way the religious fanatics policed the Sabbath and tried to segregate men and women in buses. She worried about the kind of education being given to orthodox Jewish young people. She feared for the future. She joined with Palestinians protestors at the then weekly demonstrations in the Jerusalem suburb of Sheikh Jarah against the ethnic cleansing taking place there and in doing so suffered the abuse the demonstrators received from the orthodox Jews taking over Palestinian property. I learned later that she had worked in the past with *The Olive Tree Movement* and organisation that became *Humans without Borders*, an Israeli non-profit organisation that takes sick Palestinian children from checkpoints to hospitals in Israel. She had also taken part in visits to the West Bank during the olive harvest to protect Palestinian olive farmers from settler attacks, working with *Rabbis for Human Rights*.

In such conversations the contested history of Israel comes alive and potent. The past is not left to the historians to discover. It is continuously invented and policed for in Israel the past is what gives legitimacy to the present, and disputes about it define the fracture lines of Israeli and Palestinian political life.

Israel: Disputed Legitimacy

The military and political success of Jewish fighters in creating a state in Palestine left Israelis from the outset with the need to present a moral justification for their achievement that the world would acknowledge.

The legal justification for the foundation of the state of Israel lay in the decision of the United Nations to approve the country's statehood. The problem of the moral justification arose from the manner of the struggle for an independent Jewish state and the fact that its birth was bought at the expense of the violent and well-planned displacement of over 700,000 Palestinians from their ancestral lands.

The military actions involved in this included terrorist bombings, of which one of the more decisive was the explosion on 22 July 1946 at the King David Hotel in Jerusalem, then the headquarters of the British Military Command in Palestine. It was organised by the *Irgun* led by Menachem Begin and caused the deaths of 91 people and injuries to 45. Terror actions by Jewish irregulars included the expulsion of Palestinians from their villages. At the village of Deir Yassin near Jerusalem, on 29 April 1948, that displacement took the form of a massacre of over one hundred villagers by the *Irgun Zivai Leumi* forces. This was a Jewish militia led by Menachem Begin and Yitzhak Shamir, both of whom who were later to become Israeli Prime Ministers. It is an event Palestinians commemorate annually to stand as a symbol of the *Nakba*.

The justification for the UN to approve a Jewish state in Palestine was that, because of the Holocaust, the world owed the Jewish people a debt that could only be repaid by granting them the homeland of their own. The British Foreign Secretary, Lord Balfour, protecting imperial interests in the Middle East, had promised that homeland to Jewish leaders in 1917.

By 1947 there were other strategic interests at play in this support. The new state of Israel, born of Zionist ideals and Nazi terror emerged quickly as a western ally in the region, a bulwark against Soviet influence in the Middle East and a defence against what the West saw as Arab nationalist threats to strategic oil supplies, sea routes and the political stability of the region. The conflicts over the birth and development of Israel have been a focal point of danger in world politics ever since.

For Zionists, Israel was the most important stage in an ambition yet to be fully realised: that of building a Jewish state on biblical lands. In Israel, Jews could live in security. For example, the Israeli writer, Amos Oz, recalled the night the United Nations passed the resolution enabling the creation of the State of Israel. [1] The news came on the radio late in the night. The village in which he lived in Palestine was awake. They celebrated. That night his father put him to bed, stroked his hair and told the young Amos that from this day on there would be no more humiliation of the Jews. He told his son stories of how his grandfather had been humiliated, how the whole Jewish people had suffered. It was impressed on him that from that day forth they would suffer no more.

Among some religious Jews, it was a return to their ancient, biblical homeland. 1948 was seen as a sign of the Jewish people's redemption, their return from the Diaspora, a return to favour in the eyes of the Lord. Their sense of history and religious practice is what Paul Connerton has called a 'theology of memory'. [2] Every festival, every prayer, every reading of the Prayer Book or the books of Moses reminded Jews of their link with the land of Palestine. In an ancient land, Israelis claimed and continue to claim as their own all archaeological sites that speak of the Jewish, pre-Christian presence in Palestine. The discovered remains of Masada where Jews committed suicide rather than submit to the Romans were extensively excavated in the early 1960s and which have been continuously restored since then, became a national shrine.

For European survivors of the Holocaust, it was the place to rebuild their world on new foundations. The Austrian born Jewish-American writer and Holocaust survivor Ruth Kluger in her memoir about her experiences as a child prisoner in Theresienstadt and Auschwitz made this point tellingly. [3] 'To hope' she wrote, 'was a duty'. She then explained that the Hebrew word for hope is *hatikvah*. It is the name of a song that some of those who went to the gas chambers sang because it was a Zionist hymn, now the national anthem of Israel. It was in Theresienstadt, Ruth Kluger wrote, that she learned she was Jew, a Zionist and a socialist. She was taught this by older children who knew their fate was death. 'When I ask myself today' she writes

> How and why an unbeliever like me can call herself a Jew, one of the several possible answers runs: 'It's because of Theresienstadt. That is where I became a Jew.' [4]

At the end of the war and after a period in Germany during which time she sought to forget what had happened to her, her hopes were refocused.

> I wanted to emigrate to Eretz Israel, to Palestine, and help build a country inspired by socialist ideals, where justice and humanity would prevail. But in Palestine the British had the whip hand, and they were as stubborn as ever regarding Jewish immigration. [5]

Fearful that a journey to Israel would be dangerous and likely to involve internment in transit camps, Ruth's mother emigrated instead to the United States. For many who made the same choice, Israel nevertheless remained as a great symbol of hope and of security.

For those who emigrated to Israel, hopes for a better and secure life were not always fulfilled. It has become a key theme of the emigration literature and of the vast archive of Holocaust memorialising, that many Jewish survivors found Israel an inhospitable place in which their experiences of suffering in the camps was not acknowledged. Jews born in Palestine – *Sabras* – were often critical of the new migrants. They scorned their inability to speak Hebrew. They questioned their moral fibre and failure to resist Nazi oppression and they disliked the forms of *shtetl* Jewishness that they thought the newcomers embodied.

Eva Hoffman, in her study of the second generation's experience and memory of the *Shoah*, captured this point like this:

> In Israel – the place where survivors should have met with the most spontaneous, an almost filial empathy – they were seen instead as discomfiting illustrations of that old, Diasporic oppression that Israel was trying hard to purge from the collective national psyche. In a state that was trying to create a "new man" – dynamic, hardy, resolute, able to till the soil and defend himself – the spectacle of woeful victimization was hardly destined to arouse sympathy. [6]

One consequence, she claims, is that survivors felt that they could not begin to explain to others what they had experienced. It was as if the new, secular state did not wish to be reminded of the religious East European origins of its new citizens. Indeed it was not until much later, in the early 1960s and in particular after the 1967 war, that recall of the Holocaust became a valued resource with which to strengthen the legitimacy of the Israeli state.

Jews who migrated to the United States experienced their new lives very differently to those who migrated to Israel. In America, Jews wanted to assimilate; in Israel, they wanted to assert their unique identity as Jews. Tony Judt, the British, Jewish historian noted also that American Jews were not at first too concerned about the Holocaust. [7] American and European support for Israel at this stage was for that of an ally in the Middle East against the background of cold war and great power rivalry.

The Arab world, of course, took a very different view of the new state. Israeli history is built on the idea that their state is and has been since the beginning under a constant threat from Arabs. It is that which justifies Israel's defence policies and in particular the war of independence 1947-1949. The Israeli interpretation is that the actions of those who fought that war were morally justified by the Holocaust.

For example, Yael Dayan, a Labour member of the Knesset, explained this in round table discussions with fellow Israelis and some Palestinian scholars in 1998. She argued that the Israelis cannot be reproached for what they did in 1948 'when we were emerging from one of the greatest tragedies of humanity which the world did not do much to avoid.' [8] She explained further that she felt no guilt about what happened, though she has doubts about some of the later action of the Israeli state.

> I do not feel guilty about 1948 or about 1967, but I certainly don't think of the years of occupation or of Israel's missing the opportunity for peace after Oslo, as among our finest hours ... I am very proud of the years between 1948 and 1967. However, I am upset about the last ten years of the occupation, which I regard as a missed opportunity. [9]

A central element of the prevailing Israeli view of the past is that the State of Israel was from the beginning surrounded by hostile Arab armies against which it had to defend itself. Ilan Pappe, one of the 'new historians' whose work confronted Israel with the history of its treatment of Palestinians, noted that Ben Gurion, Israel's first Prime Minister thought of Palestinians as a 'fifth column' and an existential threat to the state's security. [10] This justified for nearly two decades the imposition of military rule on Palestinian communities. Palestinians were denied rights to own property, to purchase land or to control water supplies. Strong efforts were made to *Judaize* whole areas such as the Galilee and to build Jewish only cities such as Carmiel and Upper Nazareth.

Managing the Past

The Israeli state did not leave the interpretation of history to chance. Through its ceremonies of remembrance of both ancient events like the Masada suicide or the Bar Kokhba Revolt against the Romans as well as more recent, twentieth century events like the Tel Haj battle between settlers and Arab attackers in the 1920s which Jews celebrate as the symbolic ending of Exile, the state anchors its rationale in the Jewish past.

The organizing trope is this: Ancient history good, Exile history bad. Against this background, as Yael Zerubavel has explained, a myth has been developed about the secular, national culture of the Hebrew in Palestine which was the foundation of the modern state. [11] The *Sabra* is the one who rejected the humiliation and, as some Israeli's believed, the complicity in suffering, of the forefathers in Exile.

The founding myths of the nation and the justification for its modern history have been clearly taught in Israeli schools in their history courses. An analysis of the content of those courses is revealing. Yitzhak Komen (1998) an Israeli history teacher, showed that the historical interpretations changed through time. In the 1965 textbooks, there was

> ... jubilation at the founding of the state of Israel, authentic pride in its achievements (including victory in the 1947-1949 war), and a strong sense of the moral righteousness: might and right were our weapons in the conflict. [12]

He noted they repeat the idea of superior Arab armies which casts the Jews in the role of potential victims of aggression and Palestinians, he claimed, were described as members of 'murderous gangs'. By 1990, the history books become more factual. Reference was made to the existence of Palestinian refugees but not to expulsion. There are now no 'gangs' or 'cowards'. [13]

That worried him since it was his view that 'without understanding and respect' there could be no empathy between Israelis and Palestinians. In the longer term, without that empathy, there could be no peace in the Middle East.

In Israel, there is now an open public debate about the past. Throughout its history, Israel has tried in systematic ways to erase the evidence of Palestinian settlement and villages to strip the landscape of any connection with the history of non-Jewish Palestine. It is a process that continues up to the present day.

Since the 1967 war and occupation of Jerusalem, Israeli policy has been to make a united Jerusalem the capital of the Jewish state. It is a strategy pursued through clearance, settlement and strict planning controls that prevent the spatial expansion of Palestinian settlements. All elements of what the architect Eyal Weisman calls Israel's 'architecture of occupation' have been designed to achieve the overall political objective. [14]

The state's use of history has been a powerful tool in the armoury of nation building and in the formation of Israeli political identities. It is a project that nevertheless has helped open up some lines of bitter conflict within Israeli society. For history in Israel has become a personal matter. Amos Oz, the Israeli novelist quoted more than a quarter century ago the words of a person from Haifa who had complained to him about some of his recent writings. The man told him:

> Look. For us, history is interwoven with biography. And not just from this morning. One can almost say that history *is* biography. Private life is virtually not private here. [15]

Some Israelis have questioned the state's approach to the past, as well as the beliefs of religious Jews about the historical origins of Israel and the Jewish people. Shlomo Sand, an Israeli historian, caused much angry debate in Israel over his claim that there was no Diaspora of Jews following the destruction of the second temple by the Romans. [16] His thesis is that the biblical stories of the Exodus and subsequent efforts by Jewish scholars to establish a coherent historical narrative bridging biblical myth with Jewish nationalism, is 'mythistory', a fusion of history and myth that lacks both archaeological and historical credibility.

In his most recent study, *The Invention of the Land of Israel: From Holy Land to Homeland*, he tried to show that the ancient texts of Judaism contained no concept of homeland or any idea that Jews constituted a nation. [17] Nineteenth century Zionists were the ones who fused together biblical concepts of the 'land of Israel' with a nationalist plan to acquire territory. He noted that the biblical geography of the land of Israel bears no correspondence to the territory now occupied by the Israeli state. Yet powerful interests within Israel and among evangelical Christian groups abroad, particularly in the United States, elide the two ideas. Sand's view is that this, paradoxically, is detrimental both to Judaism and to the security of Israel because it distorts Jewish theology and drives Israel to seek territorial expansion in the Middle East. This is a sure recipe for conflict and international condemnation.

'Mythistory' remains nevertheless, a potent ingredient of Israeli and Jewish historical consciousness and debate on these matters touches on all the fundamental ideological bases of the Israeli state such as the 'right' it claims, which is codified in its Law of Return, to welcome Jewish people from all over the world to become citizens.

At the same time, it opens up Zionist policies to the entirely justified criticism that the Israeli state's development is built on a fundamental flaw: the denial of the human rights and historical presence of Palestinians in the land Israel's leaders have claimed as the unique right of Jews to own and occupy.

The Holocaust

Debates within Israel about the ancient past touch deep political sensibilities but they fade into insignificance compared to the role the Holocaust has played in Israeli political culture, particularly since the early 1960s, beginning with the Eichmann trial in 1961 that brought its horrors, its 'banality of evil', to use Hannah Arendt's description of it, to full international attention. [18] There is consensus among Israeli historians that this trial was an important moment in the history of Israel, one that served to unite diverse groups of Jewish immigrants into a stronger sense of a national community with an unchallengeable right to the land they occupied.

Over the half century since the trial, there has been across the western world a growth of Holocaust scholarship and memorialising in film, oral history, literature and tourism. One critic of this, Norman Finkelestein, an American Jew and academic and child of Holocaust survivors, and now a *persona non grata* in Israel, characterised the American interests in and pre-occupation with this topic since the late 1960s – but not before then when its was not so intensively discussed – as an industry that has grown to strengthen American support for Israel. [19]

Such support played on American fears that criticism of and attacks on Israel – as in 1967 and 1973 – are harbingers of another Holocaust against the Jews against which 'our democratic ally' needs protection. Finkelstein claimed also that a focus on the Holocaust was also a way of defeating anti-Semitism in America directed at American Jews, one of the most successfully assimilated groups in the world, by evoking sympathy for them rather than resentment at their success in American society.

Israeli leaders have welcomed this support and have strengthened it. Ariel Sharon, Israel's controversial soldier-politician and Prime Minister said in a speech commemorating the 60th anniversary of the liberation of Auschwitz in 2005 that Auschwitz was the reminder that Israel is the only state in the world where Jews can be secure and have the right and ability to defend themselves. Israel invests heavily in Holocaust memorialising and this is exemplified poignantly in the Holocaust museum of Yad Vashem in Jerusalem.

Yad Vashem

Built near Mount Herzl, it is a place of pilgrimage and a vital element of Israel's collective memory and therefore a telling indicator of how the past is constructed there. Mooted after the war to recall for posterity the crime of the Holocaust, it was built in the 1950s and reconstructed in the 1990s. The present museum was opened in 2005. It is a museum, a research institute and documentation centre. The Israeli state invites all significant foreign politicians to visit the site to help them understand that the events it recalls are at the centre of Israeli national identity.

This beautifully designed, prestigious memorial is obviously more than a museum; it has become a sacred site. Nevertheless, it tells in brilliant displays the story of how ancient anti-Semitism metamorphosed into pogroms, population displacement, denial of human rights and, in German-controlled Europe in the twentieth century into deportations, camps, killings and mass murder, all driven by an ethnic cleansing programme to rid the Aryan Reich of its Jews. In Hitler's drive for a racially pure Reich and in his mad, pre-modern ideology that it was the blood in people's veins that stamped on them their national and political identity, the Jews were an obstacle to be removed, a people to be annihilated.

The final display areas cover the post-war period, the Jewish fight against the British Mandate authorities and what Israelis call the 'war of independence' that led to Ben Gurion's declaration of the state of Israel. The newsreel of his broadcast is shown here and his fine words that Israel will be a democratic state that respects human rights and lives in peace with its neighbours, no doubt fill Israeli hearts with pride.

Eva Hoffman commented:

> The intention of Yad Vashem is to commemorate the Holocaust within an Israeli context, to transport its legacy, so to speak, to the Jewish state. [20]

She found ambiguity in this. She said that the countries deeply associated in her mind with the Holocaust are Poland, Germany and 'even America' for Israel uses the Holocaust to promote patriotic feelings for Israel among Jews across the world. She noted; '... Israeli politicians were not above using potent allusions to that tragedy as a chip in a loaded game, a card meant to recharge the world's sense of obligation and guilt.' [21]

Lessons of the past

Some Israelis see the contemporary Zionist project as being a dangerous distortion of what Zionism once meant. They have noted the paradox that the policies that many hope will secure the future of the Jewish state, are those breeding the seeds of its destruction. Amira Haas, the well-known Israeli journalist regards Israel as a society living in a state of denial about its occupation of Palestinian land and human rights. [22] Of Israelis she says: they are blind to the future they are building. She believes that, unless they change, they might as well agree with the words of Samson when he destroyed the temple: 'Let us die with the philistines'.

Insofar as history has a message, the Holocaust teaches, as Zygmunt Bauman has explained, that the conditions that made it possible are those of modernity *and that they remain with us.* [23]

Guided by a grand vision of a perfect society of the future (in the Nazi case, of a Europe free of Jews), modern genocide is a planned project. It combines absolute power with rational bureaucratic action of a kind stripped of any moral consideration. This is made psychologically bearable to its perpetrators because the people they annihilate are not considered to be people. People herded into trains became 'cargo'. Bauman's conclusion to his study of the Holocaust is shocking:

> In the face of an unscrupulous team saddling the powerful machine of the modern state with its monopoly of physical violence and coercion, the most vaunted accomplishments of modern civilization failed as safeguards against barbarism. Civilization proved incapable of guaranteeing moral use of the awesome powers it brought into being. [24]

The lesson Israelis have drawn from the Holocaust is that it was a Jewish tragedy and that they will never allow another to take place. Their insurance against such a possibility is overwhelming military power. It is a stance that has been engineered to dovetail with American strategic interests in the region. Missing from it is a concern for the immorality of the abuse of human rights or of a sense of responsibility for the consequences of their achievement in building a state for those who paid a heavy price for their success.

Zygmunt and Janina Bauman's work shows there is better lesson to be drawn from the experience of Jewish survivors of the Holocaust. Janina Bauman wrote two powerful and moving volumes of autobiography about her experiences during the war and her survival in the Warsaw ghetto. She says in the Preface to the first book *Winter in the Morning: A Young Girl's life in the Warsaw Ghetto and Beyond*, that:

> During the war I learned the truth we usually choose

to leave unsaid: that the cruellest thing about cruelty is that it dehumanises its victims before it destroys them. And that the hardest of struggles is to remain human in inhuman conditions. [25]

In her second book, *A Dream of Belonging: My Years in Postwar Poland* she evokes brilliantly the ways in which Polish Jews experienced anti-Semitic attacks by the state in the immediate aftermath of the 1967 Six-Day war in Palestine. [26] The Baumans lost their jobs and regretted their support for the Communist Party.

In a very moving passage, when a Jewish friend complained to them that they (as Jews) had accepted their wellbeing in the Polish Communist Party too readily, and now was the time to pay for their blindness about what was going on around them, Zygmunt (named Konrad in the book) commented: 'The evil is indivisible. If you close your eyes when others are trampled on, you give up the right to a better fate.' [27]

It is hard not to read that as a general comment on the dangers of indifference to the needs of those who are persecuted, wherever they are. Eva Hoffman has pinpointed an important lesson from this in her survey of Holocaust history that has great significance for the Israel-Palestine conflict today. She wrote: 'neither Poles nor Jews came up with a satisfactory paradigm for combining respect for difference with a sense of mutual belonging.' [28] 'Neither Poles nor Jews found, or even theorized, a sphere of commonalty, in which they could think of themselves not as adversaries fighting for their corner but as members of one social body'.

This is a still unresolved problem. The development of the state of Israel took a form that set relations between Jews and Palestinians into a trajectory of increasing conflict, mutual resentment and incomprehension and has left only a small public space in which to explore their 'sphere of commonality'.

The Palestinian past

The experience of the Palestinians under Israeli occupation is a story, from 1948 onwards of forced expulsion from their homes, displacement, ghettoization, violence and denial of human rights. It is a story of colonization driven by a religious and nationalist ideology and its logical end they fear is clear: the ethnic cleansing of Palestine and the removal of Palestinians from their homeland to adjacent Arab states.

The Palestinian recall of the past has defined the founding of the State of Israel as *Al-Nakba*, the catastrophe. It is not an event of the remote past. Nazmi Ju'beh noted in a comment on Yael Dayan's perception of the young Israeli state being surrounded by Arab armies, that *Al-Nakba* was not over for him. [29] He was reminded of it every time he saw a Jewish settlement on Palestinian land.

The point can be generalized. Every time a Palestinian is humiliated at a checkpoint they are confronted by the past and by what they perceive as the oppressive presence of the Israeli state. On the streets of Nablus and Hebron and other Palestinians cities there are posters of pictures of 'Martyrs' killed in battles with Israeli forces. These are a daily reminder of past struggles with the occupier.

Memory has to be seen in context and in the light of the resources available to people to reconstruct it. Laleh Khalili, an Arab student in Columbia University undertook oral history research among Palestinian refugees in Southern Lebanon. [30]

Her work recovered an underlying trope in Palestinian memory: 'a sense of accelerating loss' and a sense of being 'uprooted'. [31] They responded to this in their everyday lives by recalling their past. They gave the names of their former villages to the congested quarters of their refugee camp. They kept 'village books' in which they recorded in detail the lives of their fellow-countrymen. A potent symbol of their exile that enters their narratives is that of the key. They treasure as heirlooms the old keys of their former homes. Khalili did not see this as nostalgia but, in the narrowed circumstances of their lives, it was a 'meaningful political activity'. It kept their past alive.

The lived past is a shared archive of stories of massacres – of Deir Yassin in 1948, of Kaffr Qassem in 1956, in Sabra and Shatila in 1982, in Jenin in April 2002, of siege – in Ramallah in 2002 – and of constant humiliation at Israeli checkpoints. It is narrative of air strikes, house demolitions and assassinations. It is a history that has produced a literature and which nurtures a strong sense among Palestinians of the need for revenge. It is a story of defeats – in Jordan, Lebanon with the associated sense of betrayal by Arab brothers – and of heroism among Palestinian fighters. The battle at Jenin has come to be known as the Palestinian Masada and its memory will encourage the resistance to Israel long into the future. Who knows whether it will be overtaken in memory by the Israeli invasions of Gaza in 2008, 2012 and 2014?

Since the second *Intifada* in 2000, following the Israeli Prime Minister's provocative trip to the al-Aqsa mosque complex, it is a memory bank enriched by a strong sense of resistance. The second Intifada, as Raja Shehadeh commented in his diaries of the Ramallah siege, is seen by many Palestinians as their 'War of Independence'. [32] The possibility of a peaceful resolution to the Israel-Palestine conflict will at a minimum require a deeper understanding than world leaders have so far shown of how these two groups of combatants understand and continue to learn about an interpret their past.

From past to future

Professor Tony Judt, (in conversation with Timothy Snyder), in his posthumously published book, *Thinking the Twentieth Century*, characterised the relationship between Jewish communities and the states of the Empire in which they lived (including Russia and Poland) as one of the 'interdependence of mutual ignorance'. [33] Jews lived in a controlled space in their *shtetls*. They knew little, he said of the world beyond and that world knew little of them. In this, noted Judt, there was at least some kind of symmetry. Jews clung to a coherent *identity* within Jewish culture and looked for some kind of protection from the authorities of the Empire. It was in their *interests* to do so. This did not, of course, protect them and it was this isolation that made them easy prey to ethnic cleansing as the Empire disintegrated into small nation states in the early years of the twentieth century.

The world of the *Shtetl*, as Eva Hoffman has noted, unravelled through migration during the early of the years of the twentieth century as Polish Jews travelled to America. It was destroyed during the Holocaust. [34] What remains among Jews is a powerful mixture of memory, identity and a determination that such destruction can never be allowed to happen again.

The relationship between people of Jewish origin both in the Middle East and across the world today cannot be compared to the world alluded to by Eva Hoffman and Tony Judt. Certainly, in Israel, it is Palestinians and not Jews who are forced to live powerlessly and without fully acknowledged human rights under the effective control of a state that despises and attacks them.

The '*Empire*' of the international community affords no protection to the human rights of Palestinians or redress for the injustices they have experienced. Under these conditions, Palestinians can be construed as an 'enemy within', displaced from their land, humiliated and attacked with impunity. Though victimhood and the fear of future attempts to annihilate them are key tropes of Israel propaganda and perhaps, too, something woven into the political psyche of many Jewish people, the roles of oppressor and oppressed in the Holy Land have been completely reversed for the past 60 years.

The language Judt used to describe the past is useful in helping us understand the present. There is an interdependence of *mutual ignorance* defining the relationship between Israelis and Palestinians. It is replicated dangerously among some of their fanatical ideological supporters abroad. If we debate these views i.e. the *identities*, *interests* and *understanding* that drive the current conflicts, and do so in an open, peaceful manner, then there is hope that they can be changed.

4

Israel and the practise of power

In a lecture in a London Synagogue to celebrate Israel's 60th anniversary in 2008 in a meeting chaired by the Chief Rabbi, Lord Sacks, the then British Prime Minister, Gordon Brown, described Israel as one of the 'greatest achievements of the twentieth century'. In the same week, Jose Manuel Barroso, President of the European Commission noted that: 'Both the European Union and the state of Israel were born out of the same great convulsion of the Second World War and the Shoah.' He went on to explain that despite its many challenges, the country has developed and prospered. 'We now take almost for granted impressive Israeli achievements in fields such as science and technology, industry, agriculture, education and the arts. In retrospect, we can only wonder at how all this was achieved under such difficult circumstances.' [1]

Fulsome as such praise is, it is completely eclipsed by the rhetorical heights that are reached when American presidents talk about Israel. President Obama once declared American support for Israel was 'eternal' and in his speech in Israel in 2013, he extolled the country's achievements as follows:

> Over the last two days, I've reaffirmed the bonds between our countries with Prime Minister Netanyahu and President Peres. I've borne witness to the ancient history of the Jewish people at the Shrine of the Book, and I've seen Israel's shining future in your scientists and your entrepreneurs. This is a nation of museums and patents,

timeless holy sites and groundbreaking innovation. Only in Israel could you see the Dead Sea Scrolls and the place where the technology on board the Mars Rover originated at the same time. [2]

There are, of course other voices with a different message from both within Israel and without. In October 2014, for instance, President Rivlin of Israel caused a stir at a meeting of the Israeli Academy of Sciences and Humanities by stating that Israel was a 'sick society'. [3] The theme of the conference was 'From Hatred of the Stranger to Acceptance of the Other' and the context to his remarks was growing evidence of tension between Arabs and Jews. He argued that Jews, whose experience of the Diaspora was of anti-Semitism and persecution, should be more sensitive to the dangers of incitement. He said: 'I'm not asking if they've forgotten to be Jews, but if they've forgotten how to be decent human beings. Have they forgotten how to converse?' He urged the Academy to find ways to reduce violence in Israeli society and ways to promote dialogue across differences of language and culture.

Such criticism is rarely aired in the western media. It does exist and in Israel there is a lively if limited debate about the kind of society Israel has become. This question became of such intense concern for one Israeli historical scholar, Shlomo Sand, that he chose to resign from being Jewish. His grounds for doing so are that Israel has become a 'fictitious ethnos of persecutors and their supporters' that is deeply racist without being aware of the fact. [4]

Those who seek change in the course of the Israel-Palestine conflict must take a view of the kind of society Israel has become. In contrast to the projected image of a modern, democratic society under permanent threat from enemies who will never recognize its right to exist, the view taken here is that Israel has become an oppressive militarized state organized for expansion and the further colonization of Palestinian land. The fulsomely supine support it receives from western leaders conceals from their publics a dangerous and unsupportable political reality.

Corrosive friendship

Western leaders' search for a peaceful, two-state resolution of this conflict has become more urgent as the difficulties of achieving it have increased. John Kerry, the American Secretary of state said in October 2014 (in the context of building a coalition to fight against the Islamic State (ISIS) in Syria whose fighters had recently beheaded a British prisoner) at a State Department event to celebrate the Muslim Eid al-Adha festival that:

> As I went around and met with people in the course of our discussions about the [anti-Islamic State] coalition ... there wasn't a leader I met with in the region who didn't raise with me spontaneously the need to try to get peace between Israel and the Palestinians, because it was a cause of recruitment and of street anger and agitation that they felt they had to respond to. [5]

This comment attracted a lot of criticism from the right in Israel. Reporting them, the British newspaper *The Telegraph* noted that it prompted a particularly angry response from Naftali Bennet, the right-wing *Jewish Home* party member and industry minister who said: 'It turns out that even when a British Muslim decapitates a British Christian, there will always be someone to blame the Jew'.

In a similar vein, in a visit to the United States in October 2014, his cabinet colleague, the Israeli defence minister, Moshe Ya'alon, the man who earlier in the year had accused John Kerry of a 'misplaced obsession and messianic fervour' about the peace process, told the *Washington Post* reporters in answer to a question about whether he supported the two state solution: 'You can call it the new Palestinian empire. We don't want to govern them, but it is not going to be a regular state for many reasons.' [6] He went on to explain it could only come into being if the Palestinians recognized the 'Jewish state of Israel' and it would be de-militarized. Such hubris is in no one's interests.

Though their reasons are varied, western leaders are entrenched in their support for Israel. Public opinion surveys in Europe, though not in the United States, have suggested that support for Israel among ordinary citizens has declined significantly. Israel is certainly worried by what it regards as its 'loss of legitimacy' in Europe and especially in the United Kingdom. [7] Western governments have to take a closer look at the policies of their 'democratic ally 'and at the kind of society Israel has become.

Society and politics

The politics of Israel outcrop from its past, its social divisions and above all, from how powerful groups both within and without have designed its future. Israel is a society unlike any other. It is a country without agreed borders. The Law of Return guarantees Jews anywhere in the world the right to live there. A sizeable proportion of those who do are therefore migrants from elsewhere – from America, Russia, Europe, North Africa, Iraq and many other countries. Israel has therefore a multi-national, polyglot population bound together by a religiously specified Jewish identity, even though many have no belief in God or engage in Jewish religious practices.

This background explains Israeli intransigence over and refusal to concede a key Palestinian demand: the right of return. Over two Likud-dominated decades, the balance of opinion on this has shifted to the right, towards an ethno nationalist version of

Israel that is defined increasingly not by religious identity but by its conflict with Palestinians.

The architecture of Israel's state power and its control of its Palestinian population, the West Bank and its siege of Gaza, involves military resources that have been kept, as a fundamental aim of US support, at a level above those of all potential combatant enemy nations. It involves a legal system whose laws allow 'administrative detention' i.e. detention without trial of (mainly) Palestinian opponents. It involves an infrastructure of Israeli-only roads and checkpoints that limit Palestinian mobility. It includes a security apparatus with the most sophisticated surveillance systems in the world and networks of paid collaborators. It maintains a professional army with a backup of well-trained reservists. It has a system of planning and building regulations that promotes settlements and restricts Palestinian housing. It is a state with a powerful security and counter-terrorism apparatus. This secret service has its counterpart in a press and public relations strategy which projects to the world the most positive picture of a successful democratic society permanently under threat. [8]

US financial support for Israel has played a decisive role in all these developments. Both directly through aid and indirectly through tax-deductible 'charitable' donations by American Jews to Israeli foundations, this aid has been considerable. Military support and financial guarantees represent massive support for the Israeli economy. The current agreement between the USA and Israel is for an aid budget of $3 billion per year for 10 years. Israel takes the largest share of American aid than anywhere else in the world.

Israel portrays itself as a friend and ally of the West. Behind the rhetoric, there are solid business interests with American and European corporations across the fields of information technology, media, construction and military hardware. Israel supplies the British army with unmanned aircraft (drones). Companies like Caterpillar supply Israel with bulldozers that are also used for military purposes and for house demolitions as Israel clears out its Palestinian population from land occupied since the 1967 war.

Israel is an investment opportunity for the world's major companies and is regarded by both the European Union and the Organization for Economic Cooperation and Development (OECD) as a major modern economy with appropriate legal and financial arrangements to engage successfully in global trade and business. For these reasons, the international Boycott Disinvestment and Sanctions campaign is perceived as a serious threat to Israel by its political and business leaders.

To head off this challenge, powerful pro-Israeli business interests, such as those of billionaire Sheldon Adelson in the US vigorously support Israel. [9] He is a friend of Benjamin Netanyahu and purchased a Hebrew language newspaper to support him. Paul Harris, *The Observer* journalist, reports that the businessman has given 'at least $60 million dollars' to the charity, *Taglit-Birthright* that pays for young Americans to visit Israel. He donates to Yad Vashem Holocaust museum and to AIPAC. In a similar vein, there are press reports of close political links between leading politicians like former UK Prime Minister and Quartet Ambassador Tony Blair and business and media interests in the USA such as those of the entrepreneur Haim Saban and media mogul Rupert Murdoch that are actively supportive of the Israeli government. [10] Saban funds a think-tank – the *Saban Centre for Middle East Policy*, which seeks to study the region and to promote American interests in the Middle East.

To make the point explicit: personal contacts and business deals among international political and business elites help build strong ties between Israel and the West and ensure that the public discourse remain uncritical of Israeli policies. In this way, Israel has become a strong link in a chain of connections that define the 'West' and its role in global capitalist development.

Political socialisation in Israel

The Zionist project within Israel needs more than external financial support. The narratives and identities in which it is entrenched had to be made legitimate in the eyes of Israeli citizens. One of the key mechanisms for achieving this has been education. It is the platform on which pride in Israel's achievements rests and the soil on which its people's deepest fears are cultivated. Since the 1950s the state has ensured that educational opportunities for the Arab Palestinian population would be restricted, not least to prevent Jews and Arabs being able to collaborate and to become opponents of the state. [11]

Research undertaken in Israel by the Hebrew university academic Nurit Peled-Elhanan has shown the role education has played in creating distorted, racist pictures of Israel's Arab population and neighbours. [12] In an interview with Harriet Sherwood, the British journalist who worked as the Middle East correspondent for the *Guardian* and the *Observer*, she explained that this is deeply internalised by young Israelis who are encouraged to see them as 'people whose life is dispensable with impunity. And not only that, but people whose number has to be diminished.' [13]

Sherwood quoted her as follows:

Everything they do, from kindergarten to the 12th grade, they are fed in all kinds of ways, through literature and songs and holidays and recreation and everything, with these chauvinistic, racist, patriotic notions.' [14]

Nurit Peled-Elhanan told Harriet Sherwood:

I only see the path to fascism. You have 5.5 million Palestinians controlled by Israel who live in a horrible apartheid with no civil and no human rights. And you have the other half who are Jews who are also losing their rights by the minute. [15]

This comment was in reference to a series of attempts to restrict Israelis' right to protest and criticize their government. Critics of Israeli education policy have claimed that the government is promoting Zionism and Judaism over democracy and peace. [16]

A militarized society?

On leaving school, the majority of young Israelis – men and women – are required to take up military service and to join what Israeli propaganda portrays as the most 'moral' army in the world. For most, this is something to look forward to. The French-Israeli writer, Valérie Zenatti has written vividly of her military service in the 1990s noting that throughout her later school years she had an intense pride in and determination to be part of the army. [17] Soldiers were role models and heroes.

As soldiers, young Israelis are often on the front line of the occupation and its conflicts. They control checkpoints. The go on raids into the West Bank. Many have been sent to the Negev to protect settlers who wish to clear Bedouin communities from their land. Many have fought in Israeli military actions in Lebanon, the West Bank and in Gaza. Still more have been deployed to control Palestinian demonstrators against the erection of the separation barrier. They have learned to use teargas and to undertake snatch arrests. Those who have fought in the wars in Lebanon and in the crowded streets of Gaza have seen such things that other Israelis cannot imagine. These experiences reinforce for them that they live in a dangerous political environment and that the enemy is Arab.

The experience of conflict has left many Israeli soldiers traumatised and some have joined together to campaign against the occupation. Some – the *refuseniks* – refuse to join the military forces. Some, like Valérie Zenatti, drew from their experience the need for Israel to withdraw from the occupied territories and to settle with the Palestinians but they are a minority. Those who do refuse to serve are treated harshly, often through periods of solitary confinement in military prisons. Their cases are well documented in organizations like *Yesh G'vul*, the *Shministin* and *New Profile* that encourage young people to refuse service on the occupied territories. Those who support such groups – often from a leftist, feminist background – are often arrested and interrogated by the security services. The state does not take kindly to those who accuse it of militarism.

Among a small minority of ex-soldiers, there are some who campaign for peace. The group, *Breaking the Silence* is formed from ex-soldiers who try to explain to the Israeli public that the occupation is undermining the values that should be at the centre of Israeli life. [18] Through lectures, exhibitions and publications based on the testimonies of soldiers who have served in the occupied territories, they seek to show that Israeli policies incite the Palestinian reactions the army seeks to repress. *Combatants for Peace* (formed in 2005) is a group that brings together former soldiers with Palestinian fighters to share experiences and build a better understanding across the divide of the need for non-violence and for a just settlement of differences. Such groups have not been able so far to slow down the momentum of the occupation juggernaut or to neutralise for most young Israelis in uniform the de-humanising consequences of their military work.

When the only way to interact with Palestinians is through the cross hairs of a gun sight, human beings become targets. Such work under conditions of oppression corrodes the humanity of the soldier holding the gun. Israeli observers at checkpoints have documented many cases of brutality towards Palestinian civilians.

There is ample, horrifying evidence of behaviour in combat of Israeli soldiers in the Gaza wars that can only be described as war crimes. There are, too, claims in the public domain that such work de-stabilises the mental health of some Israeli soldiers resulting in domestic violence, alcoholism and depression. For those unaffected in this way, memories of their service are of pride and the benefits of having served are significant. Ex-soldiers are helped with jobs and with scholarships to higher education so that their civilian life chances are not damaged in anyway on account of military service.

Managing the narrative

Israel has a sophisticated mass media that is dominated by right wing newspapers. It has been used intelligently by the Israeli state both at home and abroad to justify Israeli policies towards Palestinians and to frame them as being essentially defensive. Ilan Pappe has argued that the media in Israel has been closely allied with and indeed controlled by the military so that it has become 'the world's most biased and nationalist media, providing a twisted picture to their readers, viewers and listeners.' [19] It achieves this, he claims by controlling the release of information and by perpetuating in all its reports a number of myths that shape how its activities are reported. He cites for example the 'Camp David myth' i.e. that the Palestinians refused a good deal but rejected it. The second one he cites is the Intifada myth, that this was an organized campaign of terror rather than a popular uprising. Another is that Israeli military action is always defensive and 'surgical' so that state assassinations can be justified as 'focussed prevention' of terror. Running through the media, he claims, is a dehumanization of Palestinians as bloodthirsty terrorists.

So far as readers and viewers are concerned, such manipulation of news narratives, including state censorship, presents a muted picture of the Israeli military and its role in the occupation or in its attacks on Gaza. Max Blumenthal, the Jewish American journalist, reporting conversations with the *Haaretz* columnist, Gideon Levy, has noted that reports of Operation Cast Lead – the 2009 attack on Gaza – were relegated to the back pages of Israeli newspapers.

There are many examples of distorted reporting. A particularly dramatic one from the recent past concerns the Turkish owned vessel *Mavi Marmara* that attempted to take peace protestors and relief supplies to Gaza to break the Israel blockade in 2010. This boat, sailing with some well-known international pro-Palestinian supporters was attacked in international waters by Israeli special forces and diverted to an Israeli port. It caused a diplomatic storm but was reported by the Israeli press as a necessary action to prevent terror attacks describing the ship as an 'Iranian Trojan horse'. This distortion led to a breach in diplomatic and military relations between Israel and Turkey – two important US allies – that has not healed.

Blumenthal has pointed out that this news strategy has become woven even into the public rituals of Israeli life so that significant religious dates become occasions to remind people – schools students in particular – of military heroism and the permanent threats against which the state protects them. [20] Thus Passover becomes a reminder that in each generation, Jews have been threatened. Yom Ha'Shoah, the Holocaust Memorial day has a self-evident role. Memorial Day reminds them of the soldiers who have died on their behalf. Independence Day is a celebration of statehood and deliverance and victory over the Arabs. The Jewish holiday of Purim is celebrated as victory over the Persians; Passover against the Egyptians. [21] Quoting an Israeli political scientist, Blumenthal summarises this as a process of 'intense indoctrination' that is at the root of the right wing consensus in Israeli politics.

One feature of that consensus has been state support for the Zionist project of expansion of illegal settlements in the West Bank and public acquiescence in the building of the separation barrier that divides the West Bank, from Israel.

Settlements

Since 1967, Israel has extended its settlements all over the West Bank. There were settlements in Gaza but these were withdrawn for strategic reasons in 2005 against strong opposition from right wing groups in the Knesset.

Settlements are a realisation of a Zionist dream: to have Jews living in what many Israelis insist on calling Judea and Samaria. Over forty years and as a process of deliberate policy, the numbers of settlements have increased and the settler population reached about 500,000 by 2014.

Israeli military forces are deployed to protect them from possible attack and the settler movement has become a potent force in Israeli political life. Like much else in Israeli society, the success of the settlement movement depended significantly on external support. Research by Friedman and Friedman-Barthoud on the funding of settlements shows that over the past decade of settlement expansion $17 billion has been invested in them from abroad. [22] It is a flow of ideological money, funds invested to serve an ideal: the creation of permanent Jewish settlement on the historic land of Judea and Samaria. The paradox in this is that such investments have created the greatest obstacle to peace in the region and have bred resentments that will last generations.

On the ground, settlers are dangerous. In Hebron, for instance, a small community of about 500 armed settlers guarded by 1,000 (often seriously disgruntled) soldiers of the Israeli army, hold the Palestinian population of the town in a tight grip. They beat people up. In the past, they have killed Palestinians.

The most dramatic episode in this sad story was the massacre of 19 Palestinian worshippers in the Ibrahimi Mosque in 1994 by a crazed, fanatically religious settler, Baruch Goldstein, whose memory is still celebrated by his supporters.

The stealth settlement of East Jerusalem has provoked great anxiety among Palestinians who have perceived this as a threat not only to their hopes of having Jerusalem as a capital of a future Palestinian state but also to the religious status of the Haram Al Sharif and the Al Aqsa mosque. Civic unrest and murders of Jews in Jerusalem late in 2014 have been interpreted by some – including Tzipi Livni, then Israeli Justice Minister – as indications that the Israel-Palestine conflict was taking on aspects of an unmanageable religious war.

A dangerous new development arising from this has been unexpected episodes alongside the general Palestinian protests in Jerusalem of murderous 'lone wolf attacks' on Israelis. Jonathan Cook, a British writer and journalist specialised in the Middle East, argued in November 2014 that such disturbances were a consequence of the provocative nature of Israeli policies and the political isolation of Palestinians in Jerusalem. Facing what they believe to be grave threats to the Al Aqsa mosque, deeply affected individuals have acted spontaneously to attempt random killings. This has created a problem for which the Israeli security apparatus has no immediate defence. [23]

Denial and Corrosion from within

The Israeli approach to security is paradoxical. The vast apparatus of the Occupation, designed both as a land grab and defence against 'Terror' neither secures the peace and stability Israelis crave nor strengthens Israeli society within. It provokes divisions among Israelis and corrodes the values many Israelis like to believe they live by.

These issues are not at the forefront of Israeli politics. There is concern among some Israeli commentators that people are losing their interest in politics. The Israeli Democracy Institute has noted declining turnouts at elections, particularly among secular Jews. [24] The Institute claims there is also evidence of a distrust of democratic institutions and a worrying belief in the importance of having strong leaders. Orthodox Jews have a higher rate of electoral participation but their commitment to democratic values is questionable.

Israelis have been encouraged to see Palestinians as the problem and to feel that actions against them can be justified. The late Stan Cohen, the South African-British-Jewish sociologist and Professor at the Hebrew University, traced the consequences of this view to allow Israelis to believe that, for example, the torture of political prisoners is justified. He wrote of well-documented cases where IDF soldiers used barbaric methods on Palestinians only to find that there was widespread public support for them to do so. As a militarized society, Israel requires the Palestinian 'other' to be seen as a permanent threat to its integrity as a state. [25]

Social Differentiation and political ethos

The society that western leaders praise profusely and support strongly is a highly differentiated and some of the differences, especially in the life chances and social status of orthodox Jews, have paradoxical consequences for political life. The Israeli Democracy Institute at its 2011 economic conference, discussed the position of ultra-orthodox young people (who do not engage with the world of work or military service). It was noted that 20% of ultra-Orthodox men aged 35-54 were unemployed in 1979, but over 60% in 2008. One consequence of this is that, as assessed by the Van Leer Institute, 85% of the orthodox community lives below the poverty line.

This is a startling observation for it means that among the fastest-growing sector of the Israeli population, and one with the most extreme right-wing, anti-Palestinian views and among whom there are some of the highest voting rates in Israel society, political power and economic status are wholly out of line. The orthodox cannot be easily integrated into mainstream Israeli life. They cost the state a lot in terms of welfare support for they have large families and through their voting power for small right-wing parties they exercise a great deal of power. Their religious leaders often express extreme views about Palestinians e.g. that it is forbidden for Jews to rent property to Palestinians and in so doing maintain a political climate that is divisive and dangerous, not only to Palestinians in Israel and in the occupied territories, but to the long-term future of Israel as a democratic state.

The Institute for Democracy reported that over the past few years social inequality has increased. It estimates that around 20% of all Israeli families live in poverty but the figure among Palestinians and the ultra orthodox families is over 50%. The institute saw dangers in this of a weakening of social solidarity that could lead to political extremism that would reduce the prospects of a peace deal with Palestinians.

Two Israeli social scientists, Tamar Herman and David Newman have noted how demographic changes have transformed the political culture of Israel. [26] They claim a *kulturkampf* is emerging between older political elites and the rising numbers of marginalized religious groups. The *Haredim* and nationalist orthodox groups as well as the poor Mizrahi and immigrants from the Soviet Union constitute now nearly 50% of the population. The *Mizrahim* feel disenfranchised; the *Haredim* feel superior on account of their knowledge of religious law; the Russians feel a strong sense of cultural superiority and the national orthodox feel threatened by democratic values. Together, these developments have nurtured a critical mass of people who resent the democratic ethos of the Israeli state. They support right wing, authoritarian leaders who wish to press ahead with the colonization of Palestine.

The War Machine

Israel is undoubtedly a country that is modern, highly developed technologically and deeply integrated into the defence and intelligence networks of the west, particularly aligned with the United States. Its military is the most powerful in the Middle East and over the past two decades has been unleashed against forces hostile to Israel in Lebanon, Iraq, Syria and in the occupied territories and Gaza.

Israel's defense budget is $15,000,000,000 per year. It possesses nuclear weapons. This budget that pays for defence forces of some 200,000 fighters and 500,000 reservists. It is a country with nearly 400 tanks, 14 submarines (of which at least three are nuclear capable). Its air force has close to 500 combat aircraft – F15s and F16s with nearly 100 attack helicopters. It possesses inter-continental ballistic missiles. [27]

Israel is among the world's top weapons exporters. In 2012, arms exports amounted to over $7.47 billion. 50% of weapons sales are to Asia. Europe is a large customer. It is a state that has attacked nuclear installations in Syria and Iraq and has threatened to attack Iranian nuclear installations should they ever reach a point of being weapons capable.

Such military power is possible because of international support. There are clear benefits to such support for the corporations involved in the international arms trade and for the intelligence services that monitor the Middle East. Companies like the UK-based G4S collaborate with Israeli security services to supply surveillance equipment for its prisons. Within Israel, the banking and financial system benefits from the expansion of settlements through its ability to finance loans for construction. And the destruction of Gaza's infrastructure during three wars over the past eight years, gives Israeli construction supplies companies many commercial opportunities that the international community pays for through aid payments.

Over the past four decades since the 1967 war, Israel's expansion and settlement policies, together with its successful diplomacy in western societies, have created a society that bears little resemblance to the one imagined by the United Nations in 1947 or the one that existed in the minds of its many supporters throughout the early years of its existence as a state. It is not the society eulogised by western leaders for its democratic credentials or its support for western values. It still has their support, but public opinion is ahead of government policies in realising that in the wider context of a volatile Middle East, Israel is a dangerous ally to deal with.

5

Palestine: resilience and resistance

The last chapter explained how the occupation has shaped the society and politics of Israel. This chapter seeks to understand the consequences for Palestinians and the ways they have resisted it. This opens up a new kind of politics that envisages a new future very different to the one currently on offer and which will break the deadly logic of the current situation.

Being and Belonging

Israel and Palestine have this in common: both are diaspora societies. The similarities stop there. Jews across the world have a right to live in Israel, whatever their nationality. Palestinians living abroad have no such rights. Whereas Jewish communities outside Israel and especially in the USA, live safely and securely, Palestinians in the diaspora have lived for several generations often under harsh and dangerous conditions of displacement in refugee camps. Despite this, Palestinians have discovered ways to maintain their culture and identity and to keep alive rightful claims to return to their land.

Those living in Israel do so as second-class citizens; others – in the West Bank and Gaza – are trapped in the logic the Israel occupation. Their life chances over the past two decades have been constrained additionally by western-led neo-liberal economic policies. Through loans, aid donations and trading controls, these have created dependency and led to increasingly resented, growing levels of social and economic inequality. Despite the existence of the Palestine Authority, real power remains in Israeli hands. [1]

Professor Robert Wade of the London School of Economics, noted in his review of the Palestinian economy in 2014 that Israel controls all external trade. It prevents Palestine having access to the World Trade Organization. It controls customs duties, labour mobility and communications. Such controls touch all aspects of Palestinian lives prompting Wade to claim of them:

> They are so pervasive and systematic that it almost seems as if the Israeli state has mapped the entire Palestinian economy in terms of input-output relations, right down to the capillary level of the individual, the household, the small firm, the large firm, the school, the university, so as to find all possible choke points, which Israeli officials can tighten or loosen at will. [2]

The outcome is that Palestinian society has become politically divided and fractured. Nevertheless, they remain determined to resist the occupation and claim their rights and freedoms and have means to do so unavailable to the older generation. The internet has given Palestinians, particularly the younger generations, a tool to campaign for those rights that ensures that their voices cannot be stifled. The world can no longer ignore them.

Experiencing the Israeli 'other'

For over sixty years, Palestinians gave encountered Israelis as occupiers controlling checkpoints, making arrests and military incursions. For the people of Gaza, Israelis are those who imprison them and bomb and strafe their communities. Such experiences have left them all angry and without hope. In many cases, they have been left traumatized.

Following the Gaza war of 2014, a Europe Aid report highlighted the long-term psychological damage of Israeli actions on the civilian population. It estimated that 10% of the population needed immediate psychiatric help, children especially who suffer anxiety and nightmares. [3] No one knows what the long-term, consequences of such trauma will be as they are sifted and sorted into Palestinian memories and hopes. This we can be sure of: none of it will be forgotten.

Economic controls on Palestinian life are reinforced by a pervasive structure of social and political control. Many Palestinians have encountered Israelis as prison guards. Prison is part of Palestine life and society. Nearly all families have members and friends who have experience of prison either as inmates or visitors. *Addameer*, the Palestinian prisoner support organization, estimates that since 1967, some 700,000 Palestinians have been imprisoned. That is almost 20% of the population and as much as 40% of the male population. At any moment there are nearly 8,000 prisoners of whom nearly 500 will be children and about 5,000 will be political detainees. [4]

Children are imprisoned under administrative detention orders imposed by security forces. In prison, Palestinians turn to both education and politics. Many learn Hebrew and many complete their (usually disrupted) school qualifications.

Many are not so lucky. There are lots of stories from prisoners that children are denied the right to education in prisons; that Israeli policy is, in fact, as the *Addameer* group reports, organized intentionally to 'un-educate' them. Since the second Intifada, over 6,000 children have been imprisoned and many found it a traumatizing experience. As explained in the last chapter, Israeli public opinion is not tuned in to prisoner abuse issues. Stan Cohen, who campaigned against it in the 1980s in the period of the first *Intifada* characterised the Israeli attitude towards it as one of denial. [5]

Reports of prisoners appearing in the web pages of human rights groups like *B'Tselem*, *Human Rights Watch* and the *Miftah* organization, describe a world of cramped conditions, poor diet, over-crowding and harsh treatment. At the same time, they describe the ways in which prisoners resist. There have been hunger strikes. Palestinians acknowledge April 17th each year as prisoners' day. They campaign for their rights in prison and they engage in the Palestinian political process, formulating reports and policy statements. And they study.

Unfortunately, it is not only in Israeli prisons that Palestinians suffer. Since the setting up of the Palestine Authority another security apparatus has grown up, that of the Fatah-controlled Palestinian Authority. It is part of the understanding that the PA has with Israel under the Oslo agreement that it will be responsible for security in the West Bank. Many young Palestinians see this Fatah-controlled security system as unjust and unaccountable and used primarily to silence those thought to be political opponents. In Gaza in 2006, before the Hamas takeover, the Fatah-controlled security apparatus with militias under the control of the Fatah and US-supported strong man, Mohammad Dahlan, was seen by many as unjust, corrupt and oppressive.

Palestinian and international commentators on human rights have expressed concern that the Palestinian National Authority has, on account of its dubious legality and the corruption of some personnel, reacted to political criticism, with repression and human rights abuses. [6] In 2013, Amnesty International noted that the PA security services regularly arrested people without firm evidence and noted that it has credible reports of prisoner abuse including torture in Palestinian prisons. *Human Rights Watch* reached the same conclusions in 2014 and pointed out that in Gaza, Hamas is responsible for many human rights abuses. It claims there are executions and unfair trials; that political dissent is punished along with peaceful assembly and free association. Journalists are harassed and there are arbitrary arrests.

Western support for the Palestine Authority and the refusal to have contact with Hamas, believing it to be a terrorist organization, has exacerbated inter-Palestinian factional fighting, breeding resentments between opponents and their families and making it much more difficult to build civil society institutions that are democratic and accountable.

Israeli policies of administrative detention and the imprisonment of minors remains, however, a prime issue provoking Palestinian anger. Children suffer under Israeli security incursions into the West Bank. *Human Rights Watch* noted in its World Report 2014 report in the section on Israel and Palestine that children are arrested for stone-throwing, often in their homes during the night and they are processed through military courts. [7] Like many adult prisoners, they are often held without charge. These policies have touched many Palestinian families and their effect is to teach them to hate their Israeli occupiers and enemy. The surprise is that Israelis are not themselves shocked by what their state does in their name.

Sam Bahour, an American-Palestinian businessman who lives in Ramallah, has publicized the case of his friend Walid Abu Rass, a Palestinian health administrator in The Health Work Committees (HWC) who was arrested in front of his family and taken without charge to prison on 9 December 2011.

Walid's daughter, 13yr old Mays, visited her dad in prison and took with her a blanket to help him keep warm. She was not allowed to give him this and was most upset. Sam Bahour asked her to write about her visit. What she has written is a powerful indictment of Israeli penal policy and without it being her intention to do so, she exposed with the innocence of a child the full brutalizing effects of the occupation on the occupiers as well as the Palestinians they control.

Her account turns on the refusal of the guard to allow her to give her father the blanket. After explaining she had a long wait to be admitted, she writes:

> ... we got to the window where we can give the soldiers what we brought for the prisoners. I hold the clothes and stand in the row for hours. When the soldier called me I ran to the window and put every single thing I have including the blanket. He told me, "NO PERMISSION FOR THE BLANKET." I was shocked. I started asking WHY? He told me with anger, "NO PERMISSION FOR THE BLANKET!" I told him please, just this blanket. It's cold inside. He said with blunt words: "NO PERMISSION FOR THE BLANKET!" I took everything and put them back inside my bag with a sad face. There is only one thing turning in my mind, I think how really precious this blanket is right now. It is the most precious thing for my dad. [8]

She was allowed 45 minutes to talk to her dad by telephone through a glass screen. When the time was up the phones were just switched off leaving a traumatized little girl with memories she will live with for the rest of her life.

Refugee Camps

There are over 3 million Palestinians who live abroad and cannot return. They live in Jordan, Lebanon, Syria and elsewhere throughout the Arab world and in the West. In Lebanon, many still live in refugee camps and have done so since 1948. They feel powerful bonds of attachment to the land of their ancestors. Exile is a key component of Palestinian culture and identity and, as Edward Said noted, of resistance. [9] The right to return to their land is a deeply held aspiration. It is one that no Palestinian politician could negotiate away.

Exile is woven into Palestinian historical narratives and is inextricably bound to some decisive and darkest moments in the modern history of their country and people. In the camps of Lebanon, Palestinians have suffered Israeli bombing and sectarian attacks. The massacres of Sabra and Shatila in 1982 at the hands of Falangist irregulars supported by the Israeli General Sharon will never be forgotten. Nor will the massacre in Jenin in April 2002 and many others, less well-reported but catalogued in websites and memories that will be recalled for generations.

Within Palestine – in Gaza and the West Bank – many Palestinians live as people who were displaced from the villages of their ancestors in 1948. Many still see themselves as refugees and, indeed, are seen by their host communities as such.

A third group is those who have chosen to live and work abroad. In the period up to the Second Intifada many Palestinians were able to work in Israel. Many worked abroad, especially in the Gulf States. These opportunities have become much more restricted, especially after the Gaza war of 2008-9. Migrant communities abroad support their members, particularly those from their own localities. Some writers have suggested that this nurtured among them a strong nationalist outlook that was nevertheless socially conservative, especially in respect of gender relationships. [10]

It is a conservatism that has absorbed some of the elements of political Islam from the Gulf State regimes in which the migrants live and which they brought back with them on home visits. In response to their marginality in the host societies, Palestinians have placed their hopes on the creation of a Palestinian state that would respect what they regard as their socially local identities, religious faith and affiliations.

The experience of exile changes through time and is being altered by changes in the relationship between generations. Exile links

Palestinians into a shared national identity and the young ones are building this through new means of communication and art. A moving example of this is the prize-winning, poetic memoir of Mourid Barghouti, *I Saw Ramallah*. [11] This book is held together by a pervading sense of tragic loss – of place, relationships and identity – muted by the long term hope and certain belief that one day they will return to their homeland. The international community must understand that such longings have a context and are a powerful dynamic in the political culture of Palestine.

The 14 kilometre journey north from Jerusalem to Ramallah on a small bus with Palestinian passengers is a crossing between two very different worlds. Clear of the suburbs of Jerusalem, the landscape is punctuated by views of the Separation Barrier or, to everyone else in the world, the Apartheid Wall, which Ariel Sharon commissioned ostensibly to protect Israelis from suicide bomber attacks. In fact, the route of the wall takes in large stretches of Palestinian land effectively stealing it. The historical memory of Palestinians is replete with checkpoint stories of brutality and humiliation at the hands of Israeli soldiers.

The West Bank is peppered with checkpoints and there are well-documented cases of pregnant women being denied access through them, and of brides being prevented from going to their weddings. Checkpoints disrupt trade and business as well as community relationships and each day remind Palestinians of the arbitrary and overwhelming power of their occupier.

Resistance culture: humiliation into hope

The reactions of Palestinians to the occupation of their land, has been described in many ways. In the 1930s, the British described it as 'revolt'. In the 1940s, revolt turned to military opposition. Post-1967 and right up to the present, Israelis described Palestinian actions – which range from youths throwing stones, through street demonstrations, (as in the first and second *Intifadas*) to rocket attacks and suicide bombing – as terrorism. Palestinians, of course, see it all as legitimate resistance against illegal colonization of their land by Jews. One thing is clear: Palestinian resistance is inseparable from Israeli actions to enforce and extend the occupation.

People in societies living under foreign occupation invariably attach great significance to the cultural traditions and productions of their own community. Through art – poetry, painting, dance and music of all kinds, writing, scholarship and theatre – they strengthen their cultural identity.

Palestinians are intensely proud of their national traditions, their folk art, their songs, musicians and their poets among whom Darwish occupies a special place. There will soon be an arts centre named after him in Ramallah that will celebrate Palestinian culture. There is a growing Palestinian film culture, with film makers exploiting new information technology to make pictures that are finding international audiences at pro-Palestinian film festivals in Europe, the USA and Australasia.

Popular culture, especially singing, is a key element of resistance. There are many Palestinian resistance songs and whenever there is an Israeli attack public radio will play them. They are well known and politically coded. There are songs to support Fatah and others that support Hamas. Singing and listening to such songs, even in private, is an act of resistance.

A young Palestinian woman who has been very active in theatre in Ramallah and is especially keen on dancing spoke eloquently about the regular festivals of poetry, of film and dance that take pace in the West Bank. Her view was that such activity, to which many 'internationals' are invited, turn 'humiliation into hope' and enable Palestinians to 'share their bitter joy' with others.

For her, culture was a form of resistance and in her view, the work of the artists she admired was a contribution, too, to change in Palestinian society. She believed that the liberation of her country and its social transformation, especially change in the social status of women, were inter-locked projects. She was keen to develop these themes in her conversation and in her reading because she believes that resistance to the occupation cannot be successful if its basis is narrowly political.

Her own preferred cultural activity involves the Palestinian Circus School which was established in 2006. She was one of the core group of people who founded it. She believed firmly that, to quote her, it

> proves that Palestinians became stronger under occupation because they have bigger challenges than anyone else in the world, which gives them more incentive to compete and prove they can do absolutely anything. Nothing is impossible for Palestinians. The circus school, just like the freedom theatre and Jenin and Ashtar theatres, gives workshops for children in marginalized regions, in villages and in refugee camps, giving them space to express themselves and help them overcome their misery or even shock caused by an invasion or a massacre.

She made the point strongly that art 'is a more effective weapon or means of resistance since it is an international language and a more civilized means that is more welcomed by different people around the world.'

Youth in Palestinian politics

There is a new generation growing up on the West Bank and in Gaza that seems increasingly unlikely to follow the political paths of their parents and grandparents. They reject both violence and compromise on Israeli terms. They feel unrepresented by the Palestinian Authority or by Hamas. In January 2011 a group from Gaza issued a statement of their grievances that immediately exploded across the internet. Their manifesto was uncompromising:

> Fuck Hamas. Fuck Israel. Fuck Fatah. Fuck UN. Fuck UNWRA. Fuck USA! We, the youth in Gaza, are so fed up with Israel, Hamas, the occupation, the violations of human rights and the indifference of the international community! We want to scream and break this wall of silence, injustice and indifference like the Israeli F16's breaking the wall of sound; scream with all the power in our souls in order to release this immense frustration that consumes us because of this fucking situation we live in; we are like lice between two nails living a nightmare inside a nightmare, no room for hope, no space for freedom [12]

They went on to explain that their main gripe was against the occupation but they were livid, too, about Hamas and its attempts to police their thoughts and their behaviour.

Later in the same year, the Palestinian Youth Movement, which claims to represent young Palestinian people in the West Bank and Gaza and abroad, issued a strong statement against the proposal to the United nations that there should be recognition of an independent Palestinian state. [13] They claim the Palestinian Authority cannot represent the people and that its willingness to accept the kinds of peace terms the international community supports, would be tantamount to betrayal of Palestinian rights. In the longer term, these are voices that will be heard. They are becoming a potent new element in Palestinian politics able to make their views known across the world through their use of the internet.

Women in Palestine

Palestinian history has cast a special role for women. Charles Tripp, political scientist, has described women's roles in nationalist resistance movements across the Middle East from the inter-war years onwards as follows. [14] They held their families together in the face of defeat. In Palestine, during the first Intifada of 1987-91 in bodies like the Palestinian Federation of Women's Action Committees, they became active in women's groups, study circles, boycott committees and literacy circles.

Their roles were, however, circumscribed later by the Palestine Authority (PA) which, under the leadership of Yasser Arafat, delegated powers to local patriarchs and clan leaders. In Gaza, Hamas has cast women in much more traditional, Islamic, family-oriented roles and insisted on dress codes and behaviour that guarantee family honour.

The outcome is that women in Palestine have two structures of oppression to overcome: traditional ideas about women's roles and the occupation. Internet-savvy, educated young women have found ways to do this that will one day play a significant part of Palestinian resistance and social change. Gender differences of power between men and women are crucial in this respect. They are being challenged, not least because they create the conditions for domestic violence.

The Palestinian blogger, Dr. Mona El-Farra, wrote in her blog on International Women's Day in March 2011, that on account of male unemployment they have much more work to do in the home. If their men are absent – through imprisonment or death – their lives are very hard. Traditional views of the role of women constrain their choices and limit their contribution 'to the progress of the society. [15] Despite that, she explains, women are succeeding through education and work to do so. As more women have become educated and computer-savvy, they have made their voices heard.

A small but telling example of this, typical of many more, is a report in a blog by Linah Alsaafin, a young, well-known Palestinian woman from Gaza who confronted an Israeli soldier at the weekly demonstration in Nabi Saleh in November 2011 during which groups of women were throwing stones at soldiers. This is what she wrote about what she said to him:

> How many houses have you raided? How many have suffocated from the tear gas fired deliberately in their homes, how many kids have you fired at? You don't care about any of that!

> His little comment solicited the same reaction from the other *sabaya*/young women around me. We were shouting over each other, then pausing to listen, then picking up on each other's sentences with added vitriol.

> "Anyway," I added, more calmly. "These stones have a special homing device built into them; they only hit occupiers."

> Two rocks then crashed into the protective shield of one soldier standing to my right. The one in front of me was completely flummoxed.

> "Where are you from?" I asked. "Brooklyn?"

> "Fuck Brooklyn." His muddy green eyes were shocked. At that moment, it hit me. I felt so sorry for him.

> The commander then marched up. "Go back ten meters," he barked.

We stayed where we are. If we were guys, there would have been pushing, shoving, anything to provoke us and for them to justify firing from close range. But we were four Palestinian women with a few other Israeli and international activists. Never underestimate the regal wrath of Palestinian women. We will go batshit crazy on you. [16]

The wrath of Palestinian women is growing and soldiers on the ground do not know how to deal with it. Their role in the Palestinian struggle for human rights will surely increase and as it does so Palestinian society will also change.

Resistance Narratives

In Palestine, one hears constantly of many instances of personal resistance. Everyone has a resistance story. The internet enables Palestinians to tell them to the world so that it is public knowledge now that there are weekly demonstrations across the West Bank and they are growing. Those at Bil'in and Nil'in, Al Maasara, Ein Salamona and Bet Jala, Beit Umar, Nabi Saleh, Walasa and many other places are becoming known internationally. These demonstrations are in a real sense leaderless but they happen nevertheless. Israelis who reject their country's policies towards the occupied territories indeed join some.

Armed resistance is a fact of political life for Palestinians. It has a long history and some groups believe that it is the only way to deal with Israel. There have been and are many armed groups. Some like the Al Aqsa brigades or Islamic Jihad fire rockets from Gaza into Israel. They train for military struggle. They recruit from among prisoners and former prisoners and build on the anger and frustration of young, often religious men, who deeply resent the occupation and who feel that there is little hope in their lives and certainly no meaning without active struggle to resist Israel.

Those who have died in armed resistance are acknowledged as martyrs. Their photographs are everywhere in Palestinian cities. In Nablus, every corner end has a memorial to a martyr killed during the Israeli occupation of the town during the second Intifada. Martyr's pictures decorate school playgrounds and young people know about the individuals, even when their martyrdom deeds go back a long way.

Nearly all Palestinian university students have engaged in some way in resistance. It is a necessary part of their experience and has taken many forms. These cover episodes of demonstration against campus closures and 'illegal actions' to continue studies off campus. The former Rector of Bir Zeit university, Professor Gabi Baramki has written of the regular incursions of Israeli troops and of demonstrations outside the campus by illegal settlers that students have had to contend with, along with closures and curfews. [17] He recounted that students have been beaten by soldiers. They have been arrested and sometimes tortured. But they continued to demonstrate and resist peacefully. During closures they studied in private homes. They hid fellow students being sought by Israeli troops. Their acts of defiance against the occupation kept the university and Palestinian identity alive.

The story of how Palestinians make sense of the acts of resistance and of the political movements that promote opposition to the occupation is a complex one. There are tensions within it between secular nationalism and Islamism, between those who believe in armed struggle and those who cling to peaceful methods of civil disobedience. In Gaza, Hamas, the Islamist movement links the struggle against Israel with the wider aim of building a society based on Islamic principles. Hamas has been able to grow and develop by working closely with the grain of Palestinian, Muslim religiosity. Fatah is heir to the secular-nationalist traditions of Palestinian political thinking but is now compromised in the view of many for its willingness to accommodate to a negotiating process – a 'peace process' – from which Palestine has so far gained very little.

Because of this, there is a view emerging among the younger generation that a new approach is needed: one based on human rights. A young, well-educated Palestinian activist explained this position to me in an e-mail like this:

> I like to view the entire Palestinian struggle as an on-going Nakba starting in 1948 and carrying on the same and even worse policies by the state of Israel.
>
> Treating the struggle as an ongoing Nakba sheds the light on the policies of the Israeli occupation: land confiscation, house demolition, imprisonment and so on [...] So if you are to speak of Palestinian demands they are: justice, freedom, equality and right of return. These are only highlights but each covers a large spectrum of rights that are missing.

In this young woman's view, collaboration with an Israel-dominated 'peace process' has been wholly counterproductive to the realization of Palestinian rights to self-determination. Her position stands opposed to both Fatah and Hamas and to current western approaches to the conflict. She demonstrates against the occupation but has no wish to engage in the negotiations and machinations of the Palestinian Authority and its local power brokers.

The politics of peace-making the past two decades and of the parties engaged in it – both in Palestine and outside in the West – has failed. The occupation continues along with the resistance to it. New voices are being heard, new possibilities countenanced even though those with power and position cling to the old, discredited positions. The situation has become unsustainable. In Gaza, it has become much much worse and dangerous.

6

Conflict: The Gaza experience

In its violence and ruthlessness, the conflict in Gaza has been very different to that of the West Bank. Its people have reacted to it with determined resistance in which military force has played a prominent role.

Following Israel's 'war of independence' in 1948, Gaza, then under Egyptian jurisdiction, received thousands of refugees. From the 1967 war to 2005, Gaza was occupied and subject to Israeli military rule. It suffered the humiliation of Israeli settlements, collective punishments, curfews and siege. Throughout much of this time, Gaza has been defined by Israel as an enemy and subjected to regular air attacks and targeted assassinations of Palestinian leaders.

The Palestinian responses provoked by these actions, has changed over time from civil resistance to armed struggle. Despite the suffering inflicted on them, their resistance has grown stronger. For what the people of Gaza lack in firepower they are amply compensated for in their determination to survive with human dignity, in their moral courage and in growing international support for their struggle.

Since 2006, the population of Gaza has been under a siege policed by border controls, snipers, aerial surveillance and gunboats. Each of the three wars of the recent past have resulted in high civilian casualties and injuries and massive destruction of buildings and the infrastructure of services for energy, sanitation and clean water. Gaza has been left with a legacy of destruction that will take years to recover from if, indeed, recovery is possible.

It is in the mirror of Gaza that the real nature of the Israeli state stands out. The Russell Tribunal on Palestine concluded at its special session in the European Parliament in Brussels in September 2014, following 'Operation Protective Edge', Israel's attack on Gaza in the summer of that year, that Israel could be charged with crimes against humanity. The tribunal claimed the evidence was overwhelming that the Israeli actions were systematically planned attacks on a civilian population aimed at its destruction.

The cumulative effect of the long-standing regime of collective punishment in Gaza appears to inflict conditions of life calculated to bring about the incremental destruction of the Palestinians as a group in Gaza. [1]

If proved in a court of law, such actions amount to crimes against humanity and could be shown to be genocidal in intent.

The compliance of the Israeli public in support of what their military and political leaders have inflicted on Gaza is clear evidence of a society that has lost its moral compass. It highlights that Israel is a state that acts beyond international law to inflict on defenceless people military violence and collective punishments that fit all the criteria of war crimes and crimes against humanity.

The language of conflict

The Israeli 'take' on the Gaza conflict has been faithfully reproduced in the right wing global media. Its key clichés are deployed relentlessly with precise effect: 'Israel has the right to defend itself'; 'Negotiations are only possible when Palestinians eschew terror'; 'No country can stand idly by while terrorists fire rockets at its towns and cities'. 'We withdrew settlements from

Gaza in 2005. What did we get in return: Rockets!'

Concerning the charge that their actions in three wars against Hamas fighters in Gaza were disproportionate and indiscriminate, the Israelis responded with the counterclaim: 'Hamas is a terrorist organization;' Hamas sites its weapons and fighters in civilian places'; 'Hamas used human shields to protect its fighters'. 'Hamas rockets are targeted at civilians'; 'Hamas's charter is to destroy the state of Israel'. Against the criticism that IDF (or IOS – Israeli Occupation Soldiers – as Palestinians call them) soldiers were guilty of indiscriminate assassinations, Israeli propagandists replied that in the 'fog of war' terrible things happen.

Each of these phrases can be traced to the speeches of pro-Israeli politicians who have commented on the Israel-Palestine conflict. In the comment columns of newspapers like *Haaretz* or the *Jerusalem Post* or the *New York Times* or, indeed, in any of the web-based news agency outlets where reports of the conflict can be found, anti-Palestinian statements repeat these charges *ad nauseam*. The key element of all of them is a fear-driven essentialism i.e. the belief that Palestinians have qualities that necessarily incline them to anti-Semitic terror.

Gaza: image and reality

Normal, everyday life in Gaza is neither normal nor possible. 1.8 million people live in one of the most densely populated pieces of land on the globe. The majority belong to families who were made refugees in 1948. Living under siege, without work or any opportunity to travel, most are not well off. One Israeli strategist, Dov Weisglass – and this is documented – explained the aim was 'to put the people of Gaza on a diet'. [2] The Israelis have restricted food supplies to a level that prevents people from starving but which keeps their minds locked on the daily tasks of survival. The military strategy behind this is to punish the people of Gaza and to persuade them that they were wrong to elect Hamas as their government in the 2006 elections.

Social and economic conditions in Gaza became, as a result, an affront to human dignity. More than half the population is under the age of 18yrs. Unemployment stands at over 60 per cent. Four fifths of the population receives food aid. Behind such statistic are hundreds of thousands of lives blighted by ill health and poor diets and poor health care facilities. [3]

There is a history to this. Until 2006 Gaza had Israeli settlements and its economy was strangled by the occupation. Tania Reinhardt argued forcibly in her book *The Roadmap to Nowhere; Israel/Palestine since 2003* that the Israeli policy of keeping Gaza a prison was deliberate and well-planned and that the withdrawal of Israeli settlements in 2005 was a trick to fend off international criticism of Israel's policies. [4] A Palestinian friend from Gaza explained in addition that the evacuation of settlements gave Israel additional means to control Gaza that could deployed without any longer having to think of the welfare of settlers. The main one was low-level flying at speeds exceeding the sound barrier. She wrote to me:

> I remember very well that time all of us started to shout 'Stop it, we can't bear more' as our doors and window frames came out from their cement bases. Our home exterior door came out from the wall.

Adi Ophir an Israeli political theorist in the Cohn Institute has written extensively on a process he calls 'catastrophization', a process in which a powerful state can reduce its enemies to a state of chaotic survival. He sees the Israeli state pursuing such a goal in the occupied Palestinian territories. [5] As a subjective experience, 'catastrophization involves turning small events or negative experiences into wider disasters'. Ophir sees it also as a political process that inflicts humiliation, scarcity, degradation and insecurity on a population and he believes that this is precisely Israel's aim in Gaza.

The Gaza economy has been wrecked. Once, people from Gaza could cross the border into Israel to work as labourers, drivers, cooks, electricians, and mechanics and in many other occupations, but this is no longer allowed. Palestinians could export goods. President Bill Clinton opened an airport in 1998 in the southern Gaza strip to allow the export of goods and to enable people to travel, but the Israelis bombed it a few years later during the second intifada. Fishermen from Gaza could not and cannot go beyond a three-mile limit or they will be shot out of the water by Israeli patrol boats.

Each day, there are drones and helicopters flying over Gaza. A very powerful scene in the Norwegian director, Vibeke Lokkeberg's 2010 documentary film *The Tears of Gaza* which was built from footage shot (clandestinely) during the 2009 Gaza war, is of a Palestinian wedding party. The guests enjoy themselves and through the eyes of a young boy, the camera looks skywards to drones and helicopters circling like vultures overhead. At night, Israeli jets frequently fly overhead breaking sound barrier speeds to create sonic booms as acts of terror. During the day, the sound of drones across Gaza is constant and a reminder of Israeli surveillance and power.

Power supplies are intermittent because Israel bombed Gaza's power plant. Palestinian mothers have to get up through the night to do their washing if the electricity comes on. It is the same for young people who wish to recharge their mobile phones and laptops – their only means of communication with the world beyond Gaza. Water supplies are polluted because Israel air attacks have destroyed sewage treatment plants. Gaza's beautiful shoreline is a health hazard from the untreated sewage that flows into it and, in times of stress, from Israeli gunboats that shell it.

The language needed to describe the situation has to reach far beyond the cliché's of the Israeli dominated international discourse. There have been three occasions in the recent past – in 2008/9, in 2012 and in 2014 – when there has been war in Gaza. In the course of these wars nearly 4,000 people (many of whom were children) have been killed and thousands more injured. Thousands of homes have been demolished by bombs and shells. Tens of thousands of people have been made homeless. The infrastructure of the area that delivers water, manages sewage and supplies energy has been significantly damaged. Gaza's health system cannot cope with the pressures on it. People live in despair. All of this is true but words cannot begin to evoke the full horror of what the people of Gaza have experienced and continue to suffer.

Western and some and Arab leaders, especially in the military regime of Egypt, hold to the Israeli line that Hamas is responsible for these developments.

This conceals that Hamas, the party Israel portrays as an Islamist terror organization, was in many ways an Israeli creation. On the divide and rule principle, Israel encouraged Islamic factions in Gaza as a counterweight to the secular Fatah in the years before 2005.

The success of Hamas as a political party in Gaza lay in its ability to offer people something the Fatah authorities – on account of what many thought of as corruption and incompetence and unjustified collaboration with Israel – had failed to guarantee: welfare and security. Hamas's seizure of power after it was denied its electoral victory in 2006 by Israel and by western powers, was to use force to destroy the security apparatus of Fatah. Western powers interpreted this as terrorist action by an Islamist force but this interpretation is flawed since it decontextualizes the growth of Hamas as a resistance movement.

Israeli policy has been to detach Gaza from the West Bank and to separate both from the historic Palestine making a geographically contiguous state of Palestine that includes the West Bank and Gaza impossible. For this to be feasible, Hamas had to be destroyed for it carried hopes of an armed response to Israel that would threaten the collaborative *modus vivendi* that had been established between Israeli security forces and the Palestinian Authority. Israel's interest in doing this may lie in the fact that there are exploitable offshore gas reserves in the eastern Mediterranean that Israel could not exploit under a Hamas controlled Gaza strip.

Israel's strategic goals are unrealisable. In three wars, it has been unable to destroy Hamas. Years of siege may have strangled the Gazan economy but have not crushed the spirit of its people. The idea – the hope – that one day Palestinians will have a state of their own that includes at least the West Bank and Gaza, cannot be destroyed by fighter jets and tank shells. Apart from the indomitable resilience of Palestinian people, there is a limit set by global public opinion beyond which Israel cannot go. Israel already stands accused of what the Russell Tribunal calls the '*sociocide*' of Gaza i.e. the attempted total destruction 'of the essence of a social group'. The slide from this to genocide is now on the horizons of possibility and there are voices in Gaza that claim this is what is happening to them. [6]

Resilience and resistance

Despite years of occupation and siege, Palestinian society, though fractured politically in the chasm that was opened in what was a civil war in 2006 between Fatah gunmen and Hamas activists, the ordinary people of Gaza have found ways to survive and maintain their dignity as Palestinians.

Being together in families was a source of strength. People knew that if they were to die under Israeli bombardment, they would do so as martyrs and they would die together. A female student from Gaza who had arrived in the UK told me that she knew of seventy families in Gaza that had been wholly wiped out in August 2014. No one was left. She, too, spoke of near death experiences with her family as they sat in fear and darkness listening through open windows to the sounds of bombing, secure in the knowledge they would die together. It gave them strength.

Religious belief has been a powerful source of resilience. A Palestinian student from Gaza told me of his experience attending a funeral with his brother during the Operation Protective Edge war of 2014. He and his brother, along with many hundreds of others, attended a funeral of a martyr killed by Israeli air strikes. During the funeral, mourners were buzzed five times by low-flying F16 Israeli jets. He thought he was about to die. The plane flew so low he could see the pilot in the cockpit. After the funeral, he asked his brother about what he thought about during the attack. Both men agreed: they had prayed silently for death knowing that God would welcome them along with all the others who would have died as martyrs during a religious service.

The young woman mentioned is one of a growing number of Palestinians who have found ways to write about their world and to communicate their experiences across the world through the Internet and other written communications. Their writing is a form of resistance. They are able to write what one editor of a collection of their short stories – Refaat Alareer – calls 'counterattack narratives.' [7]

Their themes, as he explained, are those 'of land, of death and dying, and of memory.' [8] Each carries a counter narrative to the ones Israel projects. Stories about land – about olive trees and about particular places – establish the 'rootedness' of Palestinians to their land and their determination to contest what Israel says about who the rightful owners are.

Stories about death are a means to assert the value of life and of the need never to give up hope that there is a better life on offer. Alareer says of this act of *sumud* – or steadfastness, 'The notion of giving up, of surrendering to the occupation, to most Palestinians sounds quite repulsive.' [9]

On memory, Alareer makes this telling point:

> Because memories shape much of our world, telling these memories in the form of stories is an act of resistance to an occupation that works hard to obliterate and destroy links between Palestine and Palestinians. [10]

Armed resistance

As times changed and as Palestinian organizations began to negotiate with Israel leading up to the Oslo Accords in 1993, Hamas emerged as the force determined to carry on armed resistance. During the al Aqsa intifada of 2000, Hamas used suicide bomb attacks in Israeli cities to highlight their cause: the end of occupation and Israeli withdrawal from the West Bank and Gaza. The campaign escalated to car bombs, attacks on settlers and rockets fired into Israel.

Israel retaliated to this 'terror' with targeted assassinations of Hamas leaders in Gaza, by military incursions and later by full-scale military operations against Hamas forces in Gaza in 2009, 2012 and 2014 with hundreds of people being killed and thousands injured.

In December 2008, on the eve of the inauguration of a new American President whom its leaders distrusted, Israel invaded Gaza ostensibly to disable Hamas and its military ability to launch rockets into southern Israel. 'Operation Cast Lead' was designed to bring what the Israelis called 'calm' to Gaza. They achieved that, killing 1,500 civilians and destroying a civilian infrastructure of homes, schools, hospitals and water treatment plants. The war was condemned throughout the world. The report on the war by Justice Richard Goldstone drew the conclusion that both Israelis and Palestinian forces had committed crimes against humanity. [11]

This report, the *United Nations Human Rights Council Report on the Gaza Conflict* published in 2009, has been the subject of a massive, well-orchestrated Israeli propaganda campaign. They saw it as biased in favour of the terror organizations and criticised it for downplaying the existential threat to Israel that derives from terrorist action. For Palestinians the report was proof that Israel was a rogue state willing and capable of inflicting violence on whomsoever and when it chose to do so.

War, Distress and Undefeated hope

Military actions in Gaza have not brought Israel the success its leaders hoped for. The attacks of 2012 and of 2014 inflicted further physical damage on Gaza and killed hundreds of people but they have neither destroyed Hamas as a political organisation nor broken the will of the Palestinian people. They have provoked a growing opposition to Israel and what it stands for in Europe and elsewhere in the world – especially the Muslim world – and have prompted some American politicians to question what the payback is for their support for Israel.

Nevertheless, the siege remains. The people of Gaza have suffered greatly the consequences of bombardment and impoverishment. The Palestinian Trauma Centre (PTC) is one of the organisations that has dealt with the mental health consequences of Israeli attacks. An on-line report on its work by the International Solidarity movement noted in April 2014:

The PTC was set up in 2007 following extensive research by its founder Dr Mohamed Altawil on the effects of chronic psychological trauma on the Gazan population. The results of the research were staggering; of the 1.8million population, 700,000 were considered to require immediate psychological, social and medical assistance. The center was set up with the aim of providing free therapy, counseling, rehabilitation and preventative programmes to children, individuals and families. Incredibly they have worked with 100 000 people so far... [12]

The suffering of people in Gaza, particularly of women and children, has been movingly portrayed by the Palestinian Centre for Human Rights (PCHR) in a report on the 2012 attack, 'Operation Pillar of defence' which, in violation of all the principles of Humanitarian Law governing violence against civilians killed 170 people, including many women and children. [13] PCHR staff interviewed survivors from 12 families. Their reports of what happened when their homes were bombed are almost unbearable to read.

No summary can do justice to the power and pity of these narratives. The women spoke of death, of insecurity, fear and stress and of family lives damaged for ever. They spoke of traumatized children, of displacement, of poverty and, sadly, of domestic violence from men unable to earn the respect of looking after their families. Women who lost husbands faced and continue to face a bleak future but are compelled by necessity to be brave.

To take one example: Nesreen Arafat (aged 27) from Gaza City, lost a child in the attacks that destroyed her home. Speaking of the second attack a few days after the first, she told the PCHR interviewer:

During the offensive, with missiles falling constantly, my children felt that they were being targeted and that they would be buried under the rubble again. Now, they can't even bear the sound of thunder. Yesterday, when it was raining, they clung to me and started crying. My children are possessed by fear. I don't know how I'm going to help them move on with their lives.

I am no better than the children. I don't think I can live normally anymore. I am shrouded with fear. [14]

Her children have at least the comfort of still having a mother. The Young Palestinian writer, Rawan Yaghi, has imagined well the experience of those children – estimated to be over 300 now facing life in Gaza'a only orphanage [15] – who lost their parents in Israeli attacks. In her short story, *From Beneath*, she evokes the voice of a child coming to consciousness in the rubble of her home after a bombing attack:

I must have been bleeding, because a horrible pain started growing in my chest. The back of my head seemed to pull me down further and further with every scream I made, and I felt I had enough strength to push everything around me away. But nothing seemed to move. I desperately needed to stand up and run for my mother's warm hug. And just then it occurred to me. No one was coming to help me. There was no movement in any part of the house. I wept even harder. [16]

The mental suffering of those who have lived through such trauma may last a lifetime. Palestinians have paid a heavy price for Israel's insatiable sense of its insecurity and the wholly distorted ideas of its leaders about how best to assure it.

They do, however, have one asset that many oppressed and suffering people lack: they know the cause of their suffering. There is a well-established Palestinian narrative of the distress and dangers of occupation. It has been passed down to them through the generations. With this knowledge, they know too how their suffering must be relieved. They will come to terms with loss and humiliation by securing their freedom from occupation and their right to self-determination.

The people of Gaza know that public opinion across the world, especially in Europe, is moving in their support. They have seen concrete evidence in freedom flotillas that have attempted to break the siege. They have seen it in reports of anti-war demonstrations across Europe. They know these actions are not enough to end their suffering but without them it cannot end. The radical task is to keep up the pressure of protest and to accelerate changes in public opinion in Europe and north America. Not to do so is to be complicit in actions that will lead to further war, to death and destruction. The people of Gaza know that, too.

Gideon Levy, the Israeli journalist, explained in his reports about Operation Cast Lead that this war of 2009 would not be the last. [17] How right he was. His argument was that the moral spine of Israel had weakened; that Israelis had been dumbed down to be unable to think critically about the state's propaganda but above all, they had not been forced to confront the price they would one day have to pay for the occupation. The powers outside Israel that support it have not yet asked for that price to be paid. Until they do, we all have a moral and political obligation to ensure support for Israel's victims and to bring their oppressors to justice.

7

Human Rights: The only way forward

There is no historical inevitability for Israelis and Palestinians to be locked together in conflict. There are better choices to be made because there are people on both sides and across the world who work for a peaceful and just resolution of their differences. Such people and the groups they represent, are grains of hope for the future for three reasons.

Firstly, they expose the fact that human rights abuses in the region are not unique to it. Racism, ethnic nationalism, economic and social inequality, political authoritarianism, sectarian fanaticism, anti-Semitism and Islamophobia – all of which are at play and amplified in this conflict – have global dimensions. Secondly, they show that deep-seated attitudes and prejudices can be overcome but to do so requires changes in the social and political circumstances in which people are forced to live. The possibilities for peace will increase when support for human rights is aligned with the work of progressive political groups on the ground in Israel and in Palestine to lever the political changes needed to realise them. Thirdly, they demonstrate that a new politics requires a new imagination and, through campaigns leads to new discoveries about how the conflict can be resolved.

There are young Israelis who join with Palestinians and members of the International Solidarity Movement to protest on a weekly basis the building of the separation barrier. There are others who oppose house demolitions. Some join with Palestinian farmers to protect olive groves from attacks by settlers. There are groups that offer support to Palestinians who are victims of Israeli violence. There are bereaved parents on both sides who meet in their grief to support one another and to build hope for peace.

There are writers like Amos Oz and David Grossman who see a settlement with the Palestinians as the surest way to secure the Jewish homeland. There are journalists like Amira Hass and Gideon Levy from the liberal newspaper *Haaretz* and many academics who hold a mirror up to Israelis in ways that encourage them to re-think how they see the future of the state. There are peace activists like David Shulman and Jeff Halper of *Ta'ayush* and the Israeli Committee Against House Demolitions (ICAHD) who stand with Palestinians to resist the bulldozers clearing Palestinian homes. There are Israelis who stand as sentinels at checkpoints to monitor abuses against Palestinians by security forces.

Outside Israel, in the USA and in Europe, there are Jewish peace groups campaigning for an end to the occupation and for a peace settlement. These include *JStreet*, the American group and *Jews for Justice and Peace in Palestine*, the UK group. There are many active Jewish intellectuals who reject the logic of Zionism and who oppose the occupation. This bloc of opinion is not yet powerful enough to alter the course of Israeli political life but it has certainly amplified the political divisions of Israeli society and promoted intense discussion in Jewish communities outside of Israel about its future.

In November 2014, for example, Daniel Barenboim, the world-renowned musician who has lived in Berlin for the past quarter century added his voice to this rising volume of concern about Israel's future. He appealed to the German government to put pressure on Israel to reach a settlement with Palestinians based on two states. 'After all' he wrote:

> we are talking here about the intellectual and political future of the state of Israel. The logic is simple: Germany

is committed to the on-going security of the state of Israel, but this is only possible in the long term if the future of the Palestinian people, too, is secured in its own sovereign state. If this does not happen, the wars and history of that region will be constantly repeated and the unbearable stalemate will continue. [1]

There are Palestinians who countenance a deal with Israel that enables both peoples to live in peace. They are divided, however, in their views about how that could be achieved. The occupation has so damaged the political institutions and processes of Palestinian society that it is difficult for a nationally agreed and supported strategy for peace to be realised.

New Voices, New differences

Given that many now believe the two state solution is dead, there are voices calling for an new approach that is based either on the older, PLO-supported idea of one, secular, democratic state shared by two peoples or on a post-Zionist view of Israeli's future. Gideon Levy, the Israeli columnist and commentator who writes for *Haaretz*, has recently articulated such a vision. In his column titled 'Time to be simple-minded' on 28 April 2013, he sketched out the idea of one state and wrote this in its defence:

> At home, an egalitarian country like this would defuse most of the hatreds that bubble up from within. Arab citizens and Palestinians, with equal rights, will lose their subversive drive against the state that alienated them and dispossessed them of their rights. It will become their country. The Jews are likely to find that most of their fears were for naught: the moment that justice is established, the dangers – real and imagined – will be subdued. [2]

He is, of course, aware that this prospect is not yet on offer and that many Israelis will think it is a mad idea. He acknowledges this but then requires his readers to imagine what the alternative is, a future he sees as one of continuing, destructive conflict. If Israelis could wish for one state there would be consequences. He explains them as follows:

> The Jews will be forced to give up the dream of a national state, likewise the Palestinians. This will be the end of Zionism in its existing form, something very painful for those who have grown used to believing that it is the only way. But it will be replaced by something incomparably more just and sustainable. [3]

It is a message to be directed not just at Israelis but to those who support the existing state and its policies from abroad. The likelihood of that message being heard is small, at least for the moment. Public opinion in western societies is not sufficiently enraged about the situation in the Middle East to demand a change of approach from governments.

For the moment, it is important that there should be a stronger and livelier global conversation about possibilities for a Holy Land where human rights are respected, where people of different faiths – or none at all – can live together securely and in which differences of culture combine in new ways to nurture a cultural and scientific creativity that knows no limits. Instead of 'burning coals of conflict' there could be beacons of hope for the whole of the Middle East.

Dialogue: weak and strong versions

There are two versions of the dialogue and better mutual understanding that many plead for: the weak version and the strong one. The former, which has attracted a lot of interest, especially, though not exclusively in the USA, is to seek ways to bring Palestinians and Israelis together so that they can better understand one another. The West East Divan Orchestra (WEDO) created by Maestro Daniel Barenboim and Edward Said, is one of the most well known examples of this. It has been built on the premise that inter-cultural dialogue and understanding is a necessary condition of peace. There are many others, such as the *Seeds for Peace* programme started in 1993 to bring young people from conflict zones into residential camps where they can enter into dialogue sessions better to understand each other. Over the past decade, such initiatives have blossomed.

The international peace organization, *Peace Direct*, has listed 85 different organizations working on peace initiatives in Israel and Palestine. [4] The *Peres Centre* in Jaffa, for example, named after its founder, the former Prime Minister and President of Israeli Shimon Peres and built controversially on an old Muslim cemetery in what was once predominantly an Arab city, is

> Focused on promoting lasting peace and advancement in the Middle East by fostering tolerance, economic and technological development, cooperation and well-being, all in the spirit of President Peres' vision. [5]

A scroll through the *Peace Direct* website reveals that the majority of the listed organisations there are built on a belief in the power of personal contact as a way to build reconciliation between peoples. Only a few express any criticism of the corrosive and violent consequences of Israel's occupation and ruthless military dominance over Palestine. The evidence of an emerging ideology that shields the occupation from criticism is clear. It is in the language of their aims and objectives and in the descriptions of the practices they engage in.

The language is rich in such words and phrases as: democracy, tolerance, living peacefully, reconciliation, dialogue, empowerment, sharing of feelings, peace through conservation, peace through art, intercultural tolerance, democratic development, respect, harmony, self-control, community development and citizenship, human rights advocacy. It captures a view that the fraught and violent politics of the conflict are resolvable by well-intentioned human beings coming together to talk out their differences.

The funds for such organisations are secured to a significant degree from external international donors, especially from the United States. For example, *The Foundation for Arab-Israeli Reconciliation* in New York is a private sector organization that works with the Peres Centre to run 'Bridges for Peace' projects for Israeli and Palestinian young people. USAID has since 2004 run a Conflict Management and Mitigation programme that offers grants to bring people together 'to address the root causes of tension and instability'. It seeks to promote 'peaceful coexistence among Israelis and Palestinians and to improve mutual understanding and dialogue. Similar work has been undertaken since 1989 by *The Abraham Foundation* to promote co-existence and equality among Jewish and Arab citizens of Israel.

There are organisations that exist to promote peace by opposing the occupation. These include *B'Tselem*, founded in 1989 to promote Palestinian human rights. There is the *Coalition of Women for Peace* founded in 2007 that stands opposed to the occupation. [6] It works for a just peace and exposes through its research work who profits from the occupation and how the Israeli state supports those who benefit from its actions in the West Bank. It has exposed, for example, how multi-national companies with a European manufacturing facility for heavy demolition and earth moving equipment such as Caterpillar and Hitachi benefit from the Israeli market. Israel has no capacity for making such machines that are so critical to the occupation policies.

Ex-military men and women in Israel have made links with Palestinian fighters in *Combatants for Peace* [7] and work to end the occupation. Working on similar lines, but perhaps more focused on explaining the damaging consequences of Israeli policies on the armed forces are the organisations, *Breaking the Silence* [8] and the *Refuser Solidarity Network*. [9] *Breaking the Silence* brings together testimony from soldiers about their work and actions in the Occupied territories. Its publications and exhibitions tell in detail of the ways that the IDF terrorises and humiliates Palestinians. The individual testimonies are a catalogue of shame for any pro-Israeli supporter to contemplate.

There are other organizations outside Israel and Palestine that take a strong line against Israeli policies. *Jewish Voice for Peace*, the San Francisco based group campaigns to end the occupation. It states:

> Israel must cease its use of military force against Palestinian civilians, including attacks involving American-supplied F-16s and Apache helicopters. Moreover, Israel must stop land seizures; destruction of homes, infrastructure, orchards and farms; arbitrary arrests and imprisonment; torture; assassinations; expulsions; curfews; travel restrictions; abuse at checkpoints; raids; collective punishment; and other violations of human rights. [10]

It promotes a new approach to the conflict based on human rights and on the need engage Palestinian refugees in a debate about their right to return within international law. The website of this group lists dozens of Jewish writers and commentators and anti-Zionist organizations across the world such as the UK-based *Jews for Boycotting Israeli Goods* or the USA-based *Jews for Palestinian*

Right of Return. There exists in Europe, the *European Jews for a Just Peace*, formed in Amsterdam in 2002 from sixteen Jewish peace groups drawn from eight different European countries. [11] They came together at a conference that had the title: 'Don't say your didn't know'. Like their US counterparts, they demand an end to the occupation, the right of return of Palestinian refugees and a just peace that would include Jerusalem as the capital of a Palestinian state.

It is hard to know how effective such groups are in changing public opinion or how effective they ever could be in shifting the key elements of US foreign policy to require its ally to come to the peace table. Three things can be said with some confidence: the Zionist response to these groups is virulently critical and should not be underestimated. Secondly, there is a significant limit to how far anti-Zionist groups will go in their criticism of Israel. Thirdly, pro-Israel support in Europe is not only confined to some Jewish groups. Right-wing, anti-Islamic movements, that thrive for other reasons connected with profound social and economic changes and political alienation, support Israel and in some European states they are gaining ground.

The British National Party, for instance, claimed that it was the only UK-based party that supported Israel's 2008 attack on Gaza. In the Netherlands, right-wing leaders like Geert Wilders, are promoting support for Israel as an attack on Islam. The French National Front under Le Pen has taken a similar line. The European right-wing, once solidly anti-Semitic, is re-aligning around support for Israel since they see that country as a bastion against Islamic influence in the West. Wilders said in a recent visit to Tel Aviv that Israel was a bastion against Islamic infleunce in the West. He said: "Our culture is based on Christianity, Judaism and humanism and [the Israelis] are fighting our fight ... If Jerusalem falls, Amsterdam and New York will be next." [12] The Norwegian madman, Anders Breivik, who massacred 77 young people on a socialist summer camp in in 2011, claimed he was a great ally of Israel fighting Islam and multi-culturalism. Such views are well represented too on the American right-wing.

Jews who criticize Israel are sometimes referred to as 'self-hating Jews' by Zionists. The web-based SHIT List, a compendium of over 8,000 Jewish names and of people who have criticized Israel are described in this way:

> If anyone still wonders how the Holocaust against European Jewry could have ever happened, all he has to do is observe the behavior of today's "Judenrat" traitors. They run forth to an anti-Semitic world trying to prove that THEY are the good Jews – not those arrogant Israelis! The Truth, however, is that these radical, leftist, academic, socialist, "progressive," enlightened know-nothings are not even worthy of the name "Jew." [13]

On this list are prominent Jews like Woody Allen, Amira Haas, Ilan Pappe and, in the UK, the late Professors Tony Judt (historian) and Stan Cohen (criminologist who is accused of crimes against his people). Daniel Barenboim is described on this list as a 'pro-terror orchestra conductor'. For those who cannot bring themselves to believe the paranoid fanaticism of the Israeli right, they should read this website.

For liberal Jews in the west, Islam as a religion is not the problem but anti-Semitism certainly is. This argument can easily slide into the claim that support for Israel is an essential element of opposition to anti-Semitism. Lord Jonathan Sacks, former Chief Rabbi in the UK, said as much when in a *Wall Street Journal* article in 2104 in which he claimed that the rising tide of anti-Semitism, driven to a significant degree by criticism of Israel and its alleged human rights abuses, was a global danger. [14] He wrote:

The assault on Israel and Jews world-wide is part of a larger pattern that includes attacks on Christians and other minority faiths in the Middle East, sub-Saharan Africa and parts of Asia – a religious equivalent of ethnic cleansing. Ultimately, this campaign amounts to an attack on Western democratic freedoms as a whole. If not halted now, it will be Europe itself that will be pushed back toward the Dark Ages.

The logic of his argument leads to the conclusion that criticism of Israel is a kind of blindness to the dangers of Hamas, Hezbollah, Al Qaeda and other extremist Islamist groups like Boko Haram, that are a threat not only to Jews but to all modern democratic societies. His explanation for the rising anti-Israel (and, therefore, in his view anti-Semitic) opinions and voices across Europe is rooted in the Enlightenment doctrine of human rights. He explained his argument as follows:

In the era since World War II, the great authority has been the Enlightenment ideal of human rights. That is why the new wave of anti-Semitism was launched at the U.N. Conference against Racism at Durban, South Africa, in the summer of 2001. There Israel was accused of the five cardinal sins against human rights: racism, apartheid, crimes against humanity, ethnic cleansing and attempted genocide.

He then explained that although human rights matter, the 'sheer disproportion of the accusations' against Israel shows that it is not humanitarian concerns that drive them and this makes Jews feel uneasy.

The elision of anti-Semitism with human rights campaigners and radical Islamism is an intriguing twist to the claim that Israel's right to exist must be asserted in defence of democratic values in Europe. It is a short step from there to defend Israeli actions in the Middle East whatever they are. Israel's human rights abuses can then be blamed on the forces against which Israel has to defend itself.

Whereas the groups and political positions discussed so far represent the weak version of peaceful dialogue and have at their core a strong defence of Israel's right to exist, the strong version is unambiguously based on two foundations: on criticism of Israeli policies and actions and a politics of human rights. This position is best represented currently by the Boycott, Disinvestment and Sanctions (BDS) campaign. [15]

Started in 2005 as a call from civil society organizations in Palestine, it has grown from two premises: firstly, that the two-state solution is no longer relevant to peace in the region. Secondly, Israel does not respond to diplomatic pressure from its allies to change course. For both reasons, the pressure of international sanctions is needed to rein Israel back from its dangerous trajectory of further conflict and oppression.

The Israeli argument against this has also been deployed against successful pro-Palestinian resolutions in several European parliaments to urge their governments to recognize a Palestinian state on the West Bank and Gaza with boundaries along the 1967 ceasefire lines. Israeli politicians and supporters abroad reject such resolutions as premature. David Cameron, the British Prime Minister said of them that they are meaningless in advance of negotiations between Israel and the Palestinians to settle the final status issues i.e. borders, the status of Jerusalem, the right of return of refugees and Palestinian recognition of the nation state of the Jewish people'. [16] He was careful not to endorse the Likud position that demands Palestinians recognition of the *'Jewish* State of Israel' for that is a much more contentious and dangerous idea.

In that speech, Cameron looked forward to a two-state solution with a 'moderate Palestinian state' sharing with the Israel the responsibility of defeating the threat they both share: Islamic fundamentalism. He did not, however, spell out how he imagined the two-state solution to come about and he certainly underestimated right-wing Israeli opposition to it.

Unbalanced Dialogue

The imbalance in the political, military and economic power that describes the relationship between Israelis and Palestinians, prevents just and sustainable bilateral agreements between them. These differences are anchored in two very different sets of national aspirations that coincide with long-standing western interests. In his speech to the Knesset in 2014, Cameron spoke of the annual £5billions worth of trade between the two countries, the use of Israeli technology in the UK armed forces and its pharmaceutical products in the health service. He could have noted that the UK donates annually approximately £90 million in humanitarian aid to the occupied territories, much of it coping with the consequences of Israel's occupation policies. [17]

He looked to the future and saw 'extraordinary' possibilities for economic development, trade and job creation. Such possibilities, he explained, required a peace deal based on two states that have settled their differences and respect one another. His version of the future is one that would fit Israel and any future demilitarized, moderate Palestinian 'entity' into a neo-liberal strategy of globalization in the hope that this would bring prosperity all around and keep the Levant in the orbit of western geo-political strategy.

The European Union is the largest donor to the Palestinian Authority. In 2013 it contributed 426 million Euros (of which 168 million was for the PA). It supplied in addition 35 million Euros of humanitarian aid. There is a debate in the EU whether such aid is worthwhile and sustainable. Some critics see such 'peaceconomics' as a subsidy to Israel's occupation with little effect in changing the real roots of Palestinian economic hardship. [18] One writer, Nathalie Tocci, has argued that without political change – an end to the occupation – the western taxpayer will continue to pay a fortune to keep supporting what is essentially an American approach to the peace process. [19]

America invests heavily in Israel. Two Israeli journalists have calculated that the USA has since 1948 given £233.7 billion dollars in aid to Israel. [20] Yearly trade with Israel amounts to $45 billion (of which $18 are US exports and $27 billion are Israeli imports). [21] Currently, America is bound to an aid package of $3.0 billion dollars per year to Israel which is the largest of America's aid contributions to anywhere in the world. It is an investment that predates the 'war on terror' and has to be seen in both ideological and strategic terms. Israel is part of America's matrix of control of the Middle East and of the political chessboard beyond in Iran, Afghanistan and the Caucasus as well as the Gulf and North Africa.

Israel's occupation of Palestine is not necessarily a functional part of this overall design. It is costly. It provokes opposition and conflict. It erodes American support in the Middle East and the Israeli ally is unmanageable. President Clinton once famously commented in 1996 after a meeting with Prime Minister Netanyahu during the latter's first term of office: 'Who the fuck does he think he is? Whose the fucking super power here?' [22] Secretary of State Kerry must have felt the same given the failure of his 2014 peace initiative that collapsed under the weight of Israel's refusal to stop building new settlement blocs on the West Bank.

Western aid donors, especially those within the EU are faced with a dilemma. In the age of austerity, the costs of supporting the Palestinian Authority and in providing reconstruction and humanitarian aid to Gaza are growing and unsustainable. Without a political solution to the Israel-Palestine conflict, no amount of aid will bring about the kind of development that will head off Palestinian resistance or rein in Israeli expansion plans.

There is, however, a way out. There is a better future to be won. It builds on solidarity with those who find the existing situation intolerable and unjust. Its focus is on human rights and its guiding principle is balanced dialogue between Israelis and Palestinians. The conditions for such dialogue do not and cannot exist while the occupation continues.

8

Re-imagining the future

The argument so far is that a new approach to the Israel-Palestine conflict has four elements: a better understanding of its history and dynamics, an exposition of the interests at play in its politics, campaigns to change key policies and, finally, creative thinking to discover a future that can be different to the one currently on offer.

By the end of 2014, the future on offer, at least so far as the international community was concerned, was the two-state solution. The PA pressed this with a resolution to the UN following successful similar resolutions passed in the EU and in the parliaments of several European states. Some Palestinian critics e.g Ali Abunimah of the electronic intifada, saw this move as a retrograde step since the current version of the two state idea necessarily fails to deal with the rights of Palestinian refugees, the oppression of the Arab citizens of Israel and the status of Jerusalem. [1] This leaves the question: what kind of political arrangements would deal with these issues?

Despite international support for two states, Richard Falk, former UN Envoy to the Occupied Territories pointed out, the Israelis would never agree to it. [2] His view, after many years working in the occupied territories, was that a peaceful future depended on an Israeli renunciation of its 'ethnocratic' identity as a Jewish state rather than as a homeland where Jews live and to become a land for both people. 'The challenge' he wrote 'of living together on the basis of equality seems to be the only template that offers the parties a vision of sustainable peace.'

This chapter argues that a settlement that could bring peace demands changes in the policies of all the key agencies of this conflict to build respect for justice and human rights. It is not sufficient just to re-imagine both a new Israel and a new Palestine based on these principles. A new 'West' and a new 'Arab world' must also be discovered.

The impasse

People live in three tenses: the past, the present and the future. The past exerts a baleful influence on the relationship between Israelis and Palestinians and people on both sides look to the future in very different ways. Two main ideas have come to dominate political discourse about the future: the Zionist and the two-state solution. Though carrying powerful emotional and ideological support, neither is realistic. Palestinians would never accept the first one; Israeli settlers on the West Bank and increasingly powerful right-wing forces in Israeli politics have torpedoed the second.

In 2003, the British, Jewish historian Tony Judt, wrote an article for the *New York Review of Books* that argued that the first of these options – the Zionist one – was redundant. [3] His case was that in a multi-cultural, polyglot and inter-dependent world, Israel was an anachronism. Such a state, as many others had noted by then, could be neither Jewish (for demographic reasons) nor democratic.

The article, he later reported, caused a furore of criticism from American Jews and other supporters of Israel. Judt thought that those Americans who think critically about Israel often feel silenced by the accusation that to express such views is anti-Semitic. Israel he believed had been successful on two fronts: in 'politically leveraging guilt' (about the Holocaust and the West's responsibility for it – something Prime Minster Netanyahu reminded President Obama of when he noted that the allies did not bomb Auschwitz) and, secondly, in the 'exploitation of ignorance' about Israeli actions on the ground in Palestine. [4] For these reasons, pro-Israel supporters have been able with American and European support to maintain Israel on a steady course of development towards a future of permanent conflict.

Alternatives

This is why there are and must be discussions about alternatives. To date, they have two main foci: one concerns the impossibility of realising either side's current ambitions for the future. The other looks beyond both, sometimes to the past, sometimes to the future when new options for a reconstructed Middle East come into view.

The first of these looks ahead to disaster: to an Israel that at one extreme would be a fully-fledged Apartheid state in conflict with its neighbours. Israel would still in some sense 'win' but remain permanently threatened by enemy neighbours. Even if that fear would never have to be confronted, there would remain another: the need to live alongside a wholly subjugated and resentful Palestinian population always capable of resistance through terror.

Sam Bahour, an American-Palestinian, strongly pro-Palestinian and well-respected public figure and businessman who lives in Ramallah and a powerful voice in the *electronic intifada*, posted an internet note on this scenario, scurrilously playing on Israeli fears:

> Soon, if the current trajectory continues, Palestinians will tell Israelis: "You win! You get it all – the West Bank, Jerusalem, Gaza, the Jordan Valley, the settlements, all the water, and guess what? You get us too! Now, where do we sign up for our health care cards?" [5]

There is a Palestinian version of this dystopia: a future in which Israel 'wins' and the prospects for political self-determination disappear. Palestinians would become like the Kurds or Armenians. They would live without a state as a diaspora people in permanent conflict with Israel. No one can know the future. The best that can be done is to debate it and to confront and face up to its emergent probabilities. The purpose in doing so is to imagine different possibilities and to build support for those that promise peace.

Radical Reframing of the future

The radical task is to work to break through this impasse of the imagination and help to articulate a new, inspiring and feasible set of possibilities that reframe this conflict completely. The difficulty to face is that both of the impossible designs for the future have powerful support both inside and outside the region.

In Europe, the Israel lobby *European Friends of Israel* (EFI), has been very active in the European Parliament. It funds trips for MEPs to visit Israel and campaigns to upgrade Israel-EU relationships. This body regards Israel as an ally in the need to protect the west against the rising tide of Islam and generally embraces a neo-conservative outlook on public policy matters. [6] Along with the *European Jewish Congress* that was formed in 2009, the EFI campaigns to strengthen trade links with Israel and to neutralise anti-Israeli commentary in the Parliament and in the press.

Certainly, Israeli strategies to influence public opinion in the West are well-organised. In the UK, campaigners for Palestinian human rights have demonstrated unequivocally that BBC reporting about the Israel-Palestine conflict is generally pro-Israel. News reports about the conflict, as Professor Greg Philo has shown, invariably omit to contextualise the information being presented. [7] Tim Llewellyn, a former BBC Middle East correspondent has argued strongly that the BBC typically privileges Israeli interpretations of events and fails to help viewers and listeners to understand the political and military imbalance that defines the occupation. [8] The result is that Palestinians emerge as potential terrorists that cannot be trusted and Israel as the victim of fanaticism. [9] Challenging the hegemony of the Israeli narrative in western public discourse is one of the key levers of change for reframing the politics of this conflict.

To do so, they have to face up to fundamental questions about their own societies. To be able to look forward with hope for a new, human rights-based approach to the Israel-Palestine conflict (and many other conflicts across the world) people have to take a critical look at the values and attitudes and material supports that define their relationships with the people in the Middle East who, through the policies their governments pursue in the region, suffer most from them.

In the past, many people in western societies looked at the Middle East through the lenses of what Edward Said called 'orientalism' – an outlook of colonial cultural prejudice that constructed the 'exotic' cultures of 'the East' as inferior to those of the West. [10] Today, its dominant threads are political rather than cultural and include strong and dangerous currents of racism and Islamophobia.

Some elements within the power blocs that support Zionism have found space in the political culture of the USA to combine racism and Islamophobia with a fundamentalist Christianity that takes Old Testament prophecy literally. It nurtures unquestioning support for Israel. It portrays Palestinians as terrorists and views Armageddon as inevitable.

The political culture of western European societies is more liberal and critical than this but there are powerful right-wing forces at work to strengthen political support for Israel.

European governments and institutions like the EU are, however, being challenged now about their pro-Israel stance. In 2014, the parliaments of the UK, France, Spain, Sweden and Ireland all voted to urge their governments to support a resolution in the United Nations for an independent state of Palestine to be recognised. Across Europe during July and August 2014, there were massive demonstrations against the Israeli attack on Gaza.

Such developments have provoked US concern about Israel's future. Much to the concern of some pro-Israeli commentators, President Obama articulated this in an interview with the *New York Times* in August 2014. He said of Israel:

> To have scratched out of rock this incredibly vibrant, incredibly successful, wealthy and powerful country is a testament to the ingenuity, energy and vision of the Jewish people. And because Israel is so capable militarily, I don't worry about Israel's *survival* ... I think the question really is *how* does Israel survive. (italics mine)

He concluded by saying: 'You have to recognize that they have legitimate claims, and this is their land and neighborhood as well.'

The questions he asks are brave and pertinent. Unfortunately, his is a weakened voice in America that dares not to gainsay the powerful Zionist and Christian lobbies that support the status quo in the Middle East. European politicians are more in the grip of corporate interests than religious ones but they too, as yet, are tightly constrained to protect the status quo and to remain of service to US interests in the region. Until a climate of challenge is built up to oppose this, western policies will not change.

Back from the abyss

There is a small but growing realization that pro-Israel policies are part of the problem. There are, for example, some Israelis living in the USA who have called recently for a fundamental revision of the current support for their country. They have insisted that Israelis gain no benefit from being oppressors and in maintaining the occupation. [12] In essence, they are demanding that Israelis look carefully at the kind of society they have created for it has become dangerously dysfunctional in its approach to its future. It is a society not answering realistically the Obama question: 'how should Israel survive?'

There are Jewish groups across the world deeply worried about the kind of society Israel has become and which campaign for changes in how their governments support Israel. There are groups that campaign alongside the BDS to boycott Israel. *Jews for Palestinian Right of Return* campaigns for human rights and for the rights of Palestinian refugees to return. *Boycott from Within* is an Israel-based but international group pressing for an end of the occupation. The web-based network, *Independent Jewish Voices* has similar objectives: to press for the human rights of Palestinians and to find ways to build collaboration for peace across the current divides. On its webpage, it lists over two hundred organizations working for these objectives. There are at least 160 of them in Israel and 48 in the West Bank and Gaza. [13]

Groups such as these are international in outlook with branches in Europe and North America. It may be the case that many such groups e.g. like the *European Jewish Network for a Just Peace* (EJJP) support the two state solution. They do so, however, from a firm position of human rights and a concern for the injustice and racism of the occupation. When the Israeli, Ronnie Barkan, one of the founding members of Boycott from Within was asked whether he saw their work leading to the destruction of the state of Israel, he said:

> If we insist on equal rights for all [one of the demands of the BDS call], it will lead to the destruction of Israel. It says a lot about that Israel. Destroying apartheid was about apartheid, not the state of South Africa. [14]

A growing body of Jewish opinion across the world does not like what it sees in Israeli society. This is not a view that so far corresponds to those of western and Israeli political leaders.

Beyond the nation state

The impasse in the search for a political resolution of the Israel-Palestine conflict has been reached because two peoples, for different reasons, lay claim to the same piece of territory. Within each society, there are great differences of belief and opinion about the future direction of growth of their nations. There is not much common ground between secular, left-liberal Israelis and their religious, right-wing compatriots. Between secular, nationalist Palestinians of Fatah and the PLO and their growing numbers of politically Islamist and socially conservative brothers in Hamas or Islamic Jihad, there is no agreement about the meaning of a Palestinian state.

Changes coursing through the international order are breaking the link between territory, political power and national identity opening up possibilities for new alliances across and within all borders. In Israel, there are groups of activists actively exploring ideas once only associated with the PLO of a one-state solution to the region's problems.

An Israeli journalist, a former Zionist and foreign correspondent for the Israeli daily *Ma'ariv*, Ofra Yeshua-Lyth, has recently published a book – part memoir, part political analysis – which argues for one democratic state for both people as the only way forward. [15]

She told the anthropologist Arpan Roy in an interview that: "Fatah's slogan was we want *a secular democratic state*," and then recalled. "I remember myself as a journalist explaining that a secular democratic state is actually a call for the annihilation of Israel. Today I say the same thing. It's true, but now I support it." [16]

Her main objection is that the Israeli state has become so influenced by religion that it is no longer capable of solving the problems of Israeli society. Among the Israeli and Palestinian intellectuals such as Ilan Pappe, and Ghada Karmi who also support the one state idea, there is a shared view that the key challenge is to campaign for Israel to become a democratic state. [17] Their argument is that the right wing of Israeli politics does not wish this. It has buried the two state idea so that the key question for them now is how to protect Israel as a Jewish ethnocracy and a colonizing power.

At the Zurich conference of the One Democratic State organization in 2014, it was pointed out by platform speakers and questioners from the floor that many Palestinians are suspicious of the one state idea lest their status as second class citizens in a colonial regime would be made worse than it currently is. The argument against that fear was put by Ghada Karmi when she pointed out that Arab Israeli citizens have more rights than Palestinians living in the West Bank and Gaza but secondly, the one state idea is just that: an idea. It is something to be explored in further democratic dialogue.

Recently, a version of the two state solution has appeared that seeks to overcome the imbalance of power and inequality in the distribution of land between Israelis and Palestinians. Mark Levine and Mathias Mossberg an American professor of History and former Swedish Ambassador respectively, have proposed what they call a 'parallel state' solution to the conflict. [18] In essence, their idea is that both Jews and Palestinians can share the same land but each group can have its own political institutions and legal structures.

Their point is that in the modern world, the forces of globalization have loosened the link between sovereignty and territory. Because this is so, the land can be available to both groups without loss of either. There could be freedom of movement and trade, joint arrangements for security, agreements to manage immigration. All these elements would enable two peoples driven apart by conflict to find a basis for cooperation and the peaceful resolution of differences. Their view is that such arrangements would bring international recognition and therefore security to both people and remove a major source of mistrust between them.

The significance of such ideas is not that they represent a realistic, short-term solution to the conflict; it is that they are being discussed and disseminated at a time when international public opinion is demanding change in the status quo. Following the Gaza war of 2014, there was a significant loosening of international support for Israel. The world, if not Israeli leaders and certainly not the rampant right of Israeli politics, is open to a post-Zionist model for the future of Israel.

The ideas behind the new possibilities are justice, fairness, human rights and a growing sense of human solidarity transcending the distinctions of ethnicity, class and national identity. In the light of these and the hopes they express, the Israeli state (as well as the majority of Arab states that are its neighbours) has become a dangerous anachronism in the modern world.

Among Jewish campaigners for a just peace in this conflict there is some common ground in the belief that change is needed in order to save Israel from itself. Jeff Halper of the *Israeli*

Committee Against House Demolitions, spelled out a campaign strategy to 'redeem Israel'. He wrote that he did not believe that the policy he characterises as MEASE i.e. 'a Militarily Enforced A-Symmetrical Equilibrium' as an alternative to real peace is sustainable. [19] His hope was that Israel can be reconstructed as a democratic state for all its citizens. Israel cannot be a religious ethnocracy and secure peace.

When Halper looked ahead, his hopes for peace rested on an Israel that values Zionist culture rather than ethnic Judaism. The Middle East becomes a place where Jews, Arabs and Christians can share sovereignty and live in peace as part of a wider, European Union-like confederation that could also include Lebanon, Syria and Jordan.

He acknowledged that none of this is currently feasible. Since the alternative – Apartheid Israel – is unsustainable, this unrealistic alternative has to be debated. People do and can campaign to change Israel. There are many ways to do so: through boycott activity, lobbying, legal challenges, cultural challenges through theatre, film, art, demonstrations and specific campaigns around such issues as the Wall, arms trading, prisoners' rights, settlements and refugee rights.

The guiding thread to them all is: end the occupation.

During the British Mandate, it was possible to travel by train from Cairo to Ramle. Such a journey has not been possible for over sixty years but it is possible to imagine that the rail links could be restored. It is not beyond the prospect of belief that the economic resources of Israel and Palestine – the land, the people and the vast reservoirs of culture and ingenuity that are the inalienable heritage of two peoples open, as they are, to the wider world – could be combined in ways that would transform the whole region. Gaza could be opened to the world. Its airport could be rebuilt. Palestinians did once work in Israel. It is not difficult to imagine free mobility of labour.

In short, all the conditions necessary for the development of a flourishing, modern society that respects religious diversity and human rights can be met in Israel-Palestine. Israelis and Palestinians as we know them could then achieve a new open identity. The 'other' disappears. Ethnic differences are overcome by solidarity and the search for knowledge. This is not a manifesto or political demand or a policy; it is an exploration of an idea: that people can overcome the past and transcend cultural differences while holding to identities that are part of their heritage. It is clear, however, that with the occupation, none of this is possible.

9
Conclusions: A case for optimism

The prospects for a peaceful resolution of the Israel-Palestine conflict seem further away than ever but the need for one has never been greater. The two-state solution to it favoured by many western politicians is moribund. There is already one state: a powerful, colonizing Israeli state that controls all the territory of historic Palestine and does so by oppressing its Palestinian population. It is considered by many critics to be an apartheid state.

Illegal Israeli settlements continue to be built on the West Bank. Gaza remains under siege. The ethnic cleansing of Jerusalem is relentless. Palestinians continue to suffer the humiliation of checkpoints and discrimination and the despair of hopelessness. A younger, internet-savvy generation among them is unwilling to accept these constraints on their lives so resistance to them is increasing. It is accompanied by a growing mistrust of the Palestinian Authority and in the ability of the international community to constrain Israel's relentless project to settle and hold the West Bank and Jerusalem.

Despite that, there are grounds for hope, not least because in its misery and suffering, especially in Gaza, the status quo is unsustainable. The civil war in Syria has shifted the focus of international concern in the Middle East. This will not always be the case, not least because the future of Jerusalem is at the vortex of an anger that is growing right across the Muslim world and which threatens to graft a religious dimension onto the Israel-Palestine conflict that could render it even more explosive and insoluble.

There is a better future to be had for Israelis and Palestinians. Its outlines and principles are plain enough: to look forward to a secular, democratic, bi-national, modern state with defined, secure international borders founded on respect for the human rights of all its citizens. With courage, imagination and purposeful campaigning this idea could become over time a reality.

At the moment, it is not a realistic proposal. It is nevertheless opportune to debate it since the political realism that has shaped the Holy Land to date has led only to escalating conflicts and the prospect of a regional catastrophe that could not be contained there. To avoid that, a radical re-framing of the ways all parties to this conflict define their strategic and national interests is required.

A new approach to peace must come therefore not only from Tel Aviv and Jerusalem, Ramallah and Gaza, but from New York (in the Security Council) Washington, London, Paris, Berlin, Brussels (through the EU), Cairo, Amman, Tehran and Riyadh. For the moment, politicians in positions of power comply with an approach and within an international framework of alliances and economic policies that lock Israelis and Palestinians into the logic of wider strategic interests and conflicts.

To date, the leaders of the western world have been both unwilling and incapable of showing the courage and understanding needed to take a new approach to the politics of peace in the Middle East. They must be compelled to change if for no other reason than it is in the interests of all – particularly of Palestinians and ordinary Israelis – that they do so.

Campaigning for Change

Israelis and Palestinians have become the people they are through conflict. They have defined each other. Israeli racism and religious ideology is used to make legitimate the occupation; Palestinian nationalism tied to anger and fear about the loss of political and cultural identity and fused for many with Islamic faith in their such for justice, is the inspiration for resistance.

Like the rest of us, Israelis and Palestinians are bound together also in the global capitalism of corporations – especially its arms industries – with its degraded democracies, rising social inequalities and human rights abuses across world. They are trapped in the destructive logic of a disordered world in which great powers, now no longer locked in the Cold War, nevertheless feel they can use military power to achieve strategic aims. The delusion that links them is the 'war on terror'. Its conflicts expose the weaknesses of the UN and of an international order that leaves millions of people powerless, disadvantaged and alienated from political life.

Among the outcomes is stasis and political failure in the Middle East. Israel and Palestine cannot be viewed apart from this overarching order and the forces that drive it. This is not a negative conclusion. It highlights that the struggle for peace in this conflict is part of a wider, global struggle for justice and peace. Against this background, there are grounds for hope.

In 2011, Palestine was admitted to membership of UNESCO. In 2012 The UN General Assembly voted, against US and Israeli opposition, to confer Observer State status on Palestine. The UN announced 2014 as 'The International Year of Solidarity with the Palestinian people'. During that year several European parliaments, including Sweden, Spain and the UK, voted to ask their governments to recognise a Palestinian state. Late in 2014, the Security Council, under US pressure, dismissed the Palestinian request for full membership of the UN.

These developments have changed little on the ground but are symbolically important. They reflect shifts in public opinion across the world and are the result of effective campaigns in many countries against the occupation and revulsion at Israeli attacks on Gaza. That revulsion has alarmed Jewish communities across Europe. Many French Jews – 7,000 of them in 2014 – and fearful of what they believed to be the rise of anti-Semitism and of political Islamism in Europe, have left to live in Israel where they have been given a warm welcome by the Israeli government.

These developments highlight that the politics of the Israel-Palestine conflict and of the wider Middle East are deeply woven into those of Europe. It is in Europe's interests that its leaders should fully recognise this and be prepared to take a lead independently of the USA to promote new approaches to peace in the region.

A further point follows: public opinion is a potent force in politics. Popular pressure is a necessary though not sufficient element compelling change in how a state's strategic interests are defined. Across Europe, if not yet in North America, public opinion is no longer so strongly pro-Israel as it once was. Solidarity Campaigns have achieved much in the past two decades in shaping public opinion to be aware of the injustice they suffer and to be supportive of Palestinian rights to self-determination.

Central to this success, despite the power and influence of Zionist lobbies to neutralise it, has been the Boycott Disinvestment and Sanctions (BDS) campaign. This campaign, founded in 2004 by Palestinian civil society organisations, has grown significantly in the past decade. [1] It achieved a high international visibility and significant success in boycotting companies whose trade with Israel strengthens the occupation. It builds on tactics that were successful in the international campaign against Apartheid South Africa in the 1970s and 1980s. It makes direct appeals to trades union organisations as well as civil society groups and academic institutions. Growing links between BDS and campaigns against the arms trade, have been turning global public opinion against Israel and its policies. The success of the BDS movement is evidenced in the growing opposition to it by political leaders in

Europe and the USA (both among Democrats and Republicans) as well as in Israel's efforts to oppose it. If the campaign was not seen to be a fundamental challenge to Israeli policies, they would not give it the attention they now focus on it.

Civil society organisations covering sport, cultural activities, scientific collaboration and faith communities and organizations like Kairos have played a role in highlighting the plight of Palestinians trapped in the violence of Israeli policies. [2] So, too have medical charities like Medical Aid for Palestine. Such groups are made up of individuals whose political work and commitment to the struggle for Palestinian rights has been substantial. Some, like Rachel Corrie, the American anti-occupation activist, have lost their lives in this cause. [3]

The threads connecting these different levels of practice i.e. the international, the national, work within civil society and the commitments of individuals, are not as yet tightly drawn but they are strengthening. The work of such groups supplies the energies for change outside those of mainstream political parties. The internet has transformed the possibilities of collaboration among them.

Internet platforms like the electronic intifada, Redress Information and Analysis and Mondoweiss, together with social networking sites like Twitter and Facebook provide the means to circumvent the biases and the silences of the international news media about this conflict and its human rights abuses. [4] Israel can no longer hide behind the successes of its propaganda campaigns or rely on the silence of western news editors to keep its occupation policies out of the news.

The internet enables pro-Palestinians campaign groups to collaborate across national borders to exert pressure on bodies like the European Union. This makes accessible the voices of those Israelis who oppose the occupation as well as Jews in America and Europe who reject Zionism. Their voices challenge the public discourse of foreign policy elites and pro-Israel think-tanks that have so far set the course of western approaches to the Middle East and to support for Israel.

Despite progress in changing public opinion, the support of governments for Israel and Israeli resistance to change remain strong. The issues that divide Israel and Palestine and which are recognised as the inalienable rights of the Palestinian people by the General Assembly of the UN are still outstanding and intractable. As expressed in resolution 3236 (XXIX) they are defined as:

> the right to self-determination without external interference; the right to national independence and sovereignty; and the right of Palestinians to return to their homes and property from which they had been displaced and uprooted. [5]

At the moment, the implementation of this resolution is unimaginable and the world knows why: Israel is being driven by leaders whose long terms aims are not of peace but of territorial expansion and the ethnic cleansing of the territory it controls. The values they claim to represent and the recognition they demand – to be a democratic 'Jewish state' with a right to security – have nothing to do with Judaism, democracy or security. The Zionist project has abused each of them. The humiliation and impoverishment of Palestinians has no place in Jewish theology; Israel's claim to be a democratic state is increasingly vitiated by its actions and the occupation threatens rather than strengthens the security of Israeli citizens.

Without the ability on the part of Palestinians to negotiate on an equal basis with Israelis, the hope for a sustainable peace deal is illusory. To insist as western leaders do that a peace deal has to be agreed by the two parties and that this is the only way forward is comparable to imagining that slave owners and slaves in the ante-bellum deep south of the United States, could sit down together to work out a plan for a shared and just future for both.

The insistence by the Israeli government that it, unlike the Palestinians, is prepared for 'unconditional negotiations' is particularly specious. Israel does not negotiate; it dictates its desired outcomes by creating 'facts on the ground'. Until there is an equalisation of rights and power to negotiate, further conflict is inevitable.

Current Israeli ideas about the shape and function of a Palestinian state i.e. that it should be, in effect, a demilitarized scatter of poor, disconnected and defenceless *bantustans*, has to be strongly opposed for it can never be acceptable to Palestinians. Nor should it be so for the international community. The price paid in human suffering in this conflict has been high and the cost of failure to find peace in the region may yet be higher. Western leaders need to be reminded of what those costs are.

The costs of failure

The price paid has taken several forms. The international community has, through the United Nations, paid for the welfare of thousands of Palestinian refugees displaced from their homes since 1948 and 1967. The costs of this support remain on going. Western governments have dispensed millions of dollars in aid to Palestinian authorities to provide welfare, housing, health care and education. Millions have been spent by European states to rebuild houses and infrastructure destroyed by Israel in military operations against Palestinians only to see them destroyed again in later cycles of violence. [6] The World Bank has recently said that this cycle of destruction and reconstruction must stop. A new approach to the development of Palestine is needed, especially to war shattered Gaza. [7]

For their constant support of Israel, western countries have lost support, respect and influence throughout the Arab world. Palestinians have borne the greatest cost: in loss of lives, of homes, of land, of security and human dignity. The price they have paid in lost opportunities to develop their country, to earn income and build institutions that a modern society needs – in health care, education and welfare – and to develop the scientific and creative potentiality of their people is incalculable.

Historians in the future will surely note that Israelis too paid a high price for their success. Their state has become a pariah across the Middle East. Public opinion in Europe has been turning against Israel. [8] Israel has become an embattled enclave and a colonizing power that continually strengthens the opposition it seeks to defend itself against. Some Israeli leaders are concerned that its policies have tested the limits of its western support to the point of losing it. In the meantime, despite having the best-equipped military in the region as well as nuclear weapons, many Israelis live in a climate of fear and threat as the permanent victims of anti-Semitism and terror.

The greatest price is being paid by future generations of Israelis and Palestinians. No monetary measure could capture the costs of losing the long-term possibilities of real security, economic growth, and of scientific and cultural achievement growing from the productive collaboration of two well-educated peoples. Such a future would be a model for the whole Middle East to emulate.

True friendship is opposition

Bertolt Brecht once commented that Hitler's first victims were the German people. Israel's ethnic nationalists and religious fanatics would do well to consider this. Over 60 years Israel has moved far beyond its ostensible founding ideals to be a democratic, secular state respecting the rights of all citizens.

Israel has been encouraged in this drift to the right by neoconservative politicians in the United States in their well-documented strategies to reconstruct the politics of the Middle East following the '9/11' attack on the twin towers in 2001. [9] Israeli citizens need to be challenged to engage much more critically to question the rationale of their state's policies of settlement, territorial expansion and control of Palestinian lives. Those who do so need more support.

Until Israelis feel the cost of their compliance with their government's policies there will be little internal pressure to change them. Fortunately, the need for change has been recognised and there is a brave minority of Israelis in public life who risk vilification by saying so.

Robert Fisk, the acclaimed British journalist, wrote of his friend, Amira Hass, the renowned Israeli journalist who has exposed the horror of Israel's treatment of Palestinians, that she always explains her journalistic vocation by recalling her mother's journey being marched to Bergen-Belsen in 1944. She and other prisoners – some of whom had died on the roadside – saw German women just 'looking from the side'. Hass has lived all her life with this family story reformulating it into her work as 'the dread of being a bystander'. [10] She has come to see he conditions of Palestinian life, especially in Gaza, as 'the central contradiction of the state of Israel – democracy for some, dispossession for the others; it is our exposed nerve.' [11]

The arguments here lead to the case for a toughened stance against Israeli intransigence by the USA and other allies in the Quartet, itself a body in need of radical revitalisation. This would be stronger evidence of a genuine friendship than supine support for the current Israeli trajectory to an apartheid state and international pariah locked in endless and dangerous conflict.

How to achieve that is an open project, a matter of further analysis, debate and discovery through our political institutions, trades unions and professional bodies and civil society organisations. It may not seem like practical politics, but this is how political life works. The aim is to challenge current orthodoxies in foreign policy, to press for new policies and to stiffen the resolve of politicians to act.

The means to achieve these ends are well known: demonstrations, boycott campaigns, solidarity work, cultural events, conferences, talks, letter campaigns and creative public relations across of range of organisations to increase awareness and build pressure for change. Such actions need to be part of a coherent narrative with a coherent political rationale. For both Israelis and Palestinians and the wider international community of which they are a part, there has to be an image of a better future to the one currently on offer.

We know, too, these actions are not enough. A million people marched in London against the Iraq war in 2003 and the Blair government still joined in America's attack. Massive demonstrations in Europe to lift the siege of Gaza have not prevented Israel's aerial bombardments or opened any doors to peace. The democratic politics of persuasion and demonstration have altered the climate of public opinion across the world but have not yet been sufficient to open the doors to peace.

Future Horizons

The sufficient conditions for change leading to a long-term, sustainable approach to peace in this conflict cannot be specified in detail. They involve change in the political and economic arrangements that support the Israeli state. Israel is not a faraway place of which people know little; it is a mighty cog in a political machine that drives the global arms trade; it supplies intelligence which western leaders believe helps to promote their strategic interests in the Middle East and to help guarantee security at home. Western governments value these arrangements but they are not conducive to a long-term peace settlement in the Middle East.

A focus on development and human rights instead of one based on counter-terrorism, arms trading and oil supplies would contribute more to collective security than the policies that have been in place for the past few decades. Governments and international bodies need to be prepared to apply carefully calibrated sanctions to Israel comparable to those the have been applied to Iran or Russia that lead to a withdrawal of West Bank settlements and lifting the Gaza siege.

Credible guarantees about security are needed, together with new approaches to the Arab regimes of the region. Support for development and human rights across the region would be far more productive of peace in Palestine than support for Gulf despotisms that daily violate the democratic principles the west claims to support.

The Israel-Palestine conflict remains a stubborn element in the complex and violent politics of the Middle East. It must be resolved and that takes more than political deals; it demands imagination.

Fortunately, the alternative to current policies has become clearer. There is a growing discussion in Israel by both academics and politicians about a 'post-Zionist' future for their country. It is not widely reported or debated internationally but ideas such as these cannot just be put back in the box. The more they are debated, the more powerful they become. There is certainly a post-Palestinian Authority debate among young Palestinians. If the PA collapses, as it could, Israel would be pitched into a position it could neither afford nor control for it would surely lose the international support it currently enjoys. New ideas and grounds for hope are desperately needed.

The Levant could flourish in its respect for the human rights of all and as an area of free trade in which its different cultures interact creatively. Israel and Palestine could be beacons for democracy and development across the Middle East. Both societies have political traditions and values that are secular in which government and religion are separate. Conflicts and misunderstandings between Israelis and Palestinians, unlike conflicts elsewhere in the region, have not been based – so far at least – on sectarian religious differences.

The institutions of each could be built on hopes rather than fears. Young Israelis and Palestinians could meet together as workers, traders, businessmen and scholars. Indeed, such meetings do take place but not yet on the basis of equality. Until they do, such work merely lends a spurious legitimacy to the occupation. With equal rights to discuss matters and with unhindered, rightful access to the resources with which to implement decision, people could work on the long-term challenges of the whole region in respect of water, energy and environmental sustainability. Their interaction need not be structured, to repeat Tony Judt's telling phrase, by 'the ignorance of fixed belief' but by openness and dialogue and a critical understanding of difference.

Based on experience elsewhere e.g. in South Africa and Northern Ireland, the detailed, practical work involved in building peace may well involve Truth and Reconciliation Commissions, reparations, criminal trials, cross-border and bi-national planning commissions, the release of prisoners, international guarantees of security and development aid.

Above all, at least in the short run, it requires political courage and leadership of a high order. Without strong support from public opinion and civil society such leadership is unlikely to emerge. For this reason, those who campaign for change in the Middle East have to keep up the pressure to bring it about working creatively in solidarity with fellow campaigners in Israel and Palestine and across the world.

The work involved will be complex, laborious and frustrating with many setbacks. Human rights should be the guiding principles of it but the inspiration needs stronger nourishment. Maybe the Palestinian poet, Mahmoud Darwish, found it with the words:

> When the planes fly off
> The doves fly back

'But', the cynical realist will say 'what happens then?' Playing the Devil's Advocate, the cynic will press further: 'How, given all that has happened, can Israelis and Palestinians live together in security and mutual respect?' 'People will not give up what they have gained or forgive those who have caused their loss and distress!' 'Can anyone seriously believe that the Jewish people can give up their homeland after all they have suffered to regain it?' The realist case then slides into fatalism: there is no solution. What will be, will be.

Such views are common, dangerous and complacent. The plight of people living under the Israeli occupation, especially those sheltering in bomb sites in Gaza, is not sustainable. What Israeli propagandists call 'calm' is merely a temporary halt to hostilities. Behind their separation barrier and under the protection of their Iron Dome missile system with nuclear weapons in reserve, Israelis may feel secure, but they live in the safety of the bomb shelter.

A significant and vocal constituency among them lives inside the illusions of the fanatic believing that one day Israel will be free of Palestinians once and for all. It can be given a name: the Lieberman illusion. It is that of the Israeli politician, Avigdor Lieberman whose ultra nationalist party, *Yisrael Beiteinu*, looks forward to the displacement of Palestinians from Israel to a de-militarised West Bank and to Jordan where, as Arabs, they can live in their own state. That would leave Israel as a 'Jewish state'. No Palestinian could ever accept that.

It was once possible to say with authority that the tragedy of the Israel-Palestine conflict had a clear, but painful solution: two states living side by side. Amoz Oz, the Israeli novelist, in his 2002 essay 'Between right and right' noted the justice behind the irreconcilable national claims of both Israel and Palestine to the same land and argued that a common interest in peace should override both and seal an agreement to live as divorced couples do, i.e. separately. Israelis would have to give up their security, since Palestine could become a base for Arab attacks on Israel, and Palestinians their right of return and that this 'is going to hurt like hell'. [12] His view was that the pay-off – peace - would be worth it. He put it this way:

> You no longer have to choose between being pro-Israel and pro-Palestine. You have to be pro-peace. [13]

It reads well but thirteen years on from its publication the hopes it expresses about two states are no longer realisable. The Israeli fears to which Oz alludes, cultivated by a leadership that refers constantly to Palestinian terror, to the threat from Hamas in Gaza and Hezbollah in Lebanon and the dark, existential threat of a nuclear-armed Iran, have not lessened. Western support has not assuaged them. Indeed, in the context of American diplomatic efforts to find a workable agreement with Iran over its nuclear programme, Israeli concerns about that country have amplified.

Hope over Fear

In the specific circumstances of the Israel-Palestine conflict, the grounds for hope and the rationale for a new kind of politics are clear. American policies towards the Middle East and tolerance of Israel's actions in the region are changing. Public opinion in the US, once strongly supportive of Israel is loosening. The EU has become much more critical of Israeli settlement policies and more prepared to express it through toughened attitudes to trading agreements. In the councils of the UN, Israel feels isolated and traduced. Increased global support for the BDS campaign – including academic and cultural boycotts – worries Israelis. Divisions within Israeli society between rich and poor, the religious and the secular, between Ashkenazi and Sephardic Jews have raised concerns about the long-tem stability of the state and its capacity to adapt to a changing environment and remain a modern, economically successful society.

Young people in Israel have shown that they are not compliant Zionists. In 2011, as the 'Arab Spring' brought down dictatorial regimes in Tunisia and Egypt, thousands of young people in Tel Aviv began tent-camp protests against rising inequalities and the high cost of housing in Israel. This 'July 14th' movement did not focus on the Palestinian question but it did expose a growing cultural fracture in Israel: that between middle class, secular Israelis and ultra-orthodox religious groups and settlers who are increasingly resented for the financial burden they impose on the state. [14] Young Israelis have much to gain from a reduction of the heavy fiscal burdens of Israel's defence budget and a small but potentially strong constituency among them looks forward to a new and different settlement with the Palestinians.

A younger generation of Palestinians is emerging to political maturity. They are well educated, modern in outlook, acutely aware of the weaknesses of their own society and its leaders and determined to share the benefits of modernity. Many have studied or seek to study abroad. Many are religious – both Muslim and Christian – but see their faith as a private matter and not something that defines their citizenship. They feel acutely the denial of their human rights and seek a future in which their freedom can be respected. They are actively engaged in the civic life of their communities working, even while studying, as volunteers in literacy projects, women's groups, arts, music and theatre groups. They have a strong sense of the needs of their society to develop and they are acutely aware of its poverties and potentialities. These are concerns, hopes and dreams that correspond precisely with those of young Israelis.

While western leaders cling to the long lost idea of a two state solution to the problems facing both peoples and while many Israelis, particularly on the right-wing of political life, insist that physical separation of Jews and Arabs is the only way forward to Jewish security, there is another option staring them in the face. It is that of a bi-national, secular, democratic state built on respect for human rights living in peace with its neighbours and contributing constructively the development of the whole Middle East.

The optimum conditions for achieving that are in Israel and Palestine. But they cannot choose to do so alone. International guarantees of security will be needed to set Israelis and Palestinians on the road to peace. No time limits can be placed on the new journey to a different future. The road ahead must be cleared of the occupation, the Gaza siege, the discrimination against Palestinians, checkpoints, administrative detentions and the poverties of underdevelopment. Palestinians need the chance to live as citizens with rights to choose their representatives and to shape the policies that govern their security and their futures. These are the means to remove the fears, the suspicions and the hatreds that have distorted the development of both societies.

This journey has its risks. The risks involved in not undertaking it are much greater. The need to continue the journey is not one for Israelis and Palestinians alone. People in the United States and Europe and across the Arab world need to join them and to compel their leaders to follow them. Their common enemies thrive in the status quo; the time has come to open up some new realities.

'What is now proved was once only imagin'd'.
William Blake, *Proverbs of He*

Endnotes

Chapter 1

1 Mansfield, Peter. 1979. The Arabs, Pelican Books, Harmondsworth p200
2 Weir, Alison. 2014. Against Our Better Judgement: How the US was used to create Israel, isbn- 13:978-1495910920
3 Achar, Gilbert. 2011. The Arabs and the Holocaust: The Arab-Israeli war of narratives, Saqi London
4 ibid p 21
5 Hobsbawm, Eric. 1994. The Age of Extremes: 1914-1991, Abacus, London
6 Brecht, Bertolt. 1935. Fünf Schwierigkeiten beim Schreiben der Wahrheit (Five difficulties in writing the Truth)

Chapter 2

1 Aneuran Bevan, Michael Foot, Gordon Brown and Tony Blair [and also most of the European left until 1967] are among Labour leaders in the UK who have publicly announced their support for Israel.
2 Sand, Shlomo. 2012. The Invention of the Land of Israel; From Holy Land to Homeland. Verso, London p 29
3 Moshe Dayan, the Israeli defence minister at the time of the Six Day War said that the army had reunited Jerusalem. 'We have returned to our holiest places, we have returned in order not to part from them ever again'. See Avi Shlaim, 2000 The Iron Wall: Israel and the Arab World. Penguin Books London p245. See also Karen Armstrong, 2007. The Bible: The biography, Atlantic books, London. P213-214. She reports

a plot in the 1980s by a group of religious Zionists following Rabbi Zvi Yehuda Kook (1891-1982)who sought to destroy Muslim structures on the Temple Mount

4   Berger, John. Undefeated Despair (https://www.opendemocracy.net/conflict-vision_reflections/palestine_3176.jsp)

5   Tripp, Charles. 2013. The Power and the People: Paths of Resistance in the Middle East. Cambridge University Press, Cambridge p 38

6   Barsamain, David and Said, Edward W. 2003. Culture and Resistance Conversations with Edward W. Pluto Press, London p159

7   Kummerling, Baruch. 2003. Politicide: Ariel Sharon's War Against the Palestinians. Verso, London

8   Barak, Ehud. quoted in Inside the Germany-Israel Relationship http://www.momentmag.com/inside-germanyisrael-relationship/ May/June 2014

9   Bauman, Zygmunt. 1989. Modernity and the Holocaust. Polity Press, Oxford

10 Bauman, Zygmunt. 2000. Liquid Modernity. Polity Press, Oxford

11 Grant, Linda. 2006. The People on the Street: A writer's view of Israel. Virago, London p197

12 Freedland, Jonathan. 2011, The Guardian April 20th

13 Judt, Tony (with Timothy Snyder). 2012. Thinking the Twentieth Century. William Heinemann, London p 126

Chapter 3

1   Oz, Amos. 2004. A Tale of Love and Darkness. Chatto and Windus, London

2   Connerton, Paul. 1989. How Societies Remember. Cambridge University Press, Cambridge p46

3   Kluger, Ruth. 2003. Landscapes of Memory: A Holocaust Girlhood Remembered. Bloomsbury, London p101

4   ibid p 98

5   ibid p 194

6 Hoffman, Eva. 2004. After Such Knowledge: A Meditation on the Aftermath of the Holocaust. Secker and Warburg, London p84

7 Judt, Tony (with Timothy Snyder). 2012 Thinking the Twentieth Century. William Heinemann, London

8 Dayan, Yael. 1998. in 'A Roundtable Discussion in the Eyes of Two Peoples 'in Palestine-Israel Journal of Politics, Economics and Culture Vol V No 2 pp 23-24)

9 ibid p 23

10 Pappe, Ilan, 2011 The Forgotten Palestinians: A history of the Palestinians in Israel. Yale University Press, New Haven and London

11 Zerubavel, Yael. 1995. Recovered Roots: Collective Memory and the Making of Israeli National Tradition. University of Chicago Press, Chicago

12 Komen, Yitzhak.1998. 'Steps Along a Winding Road: The Changing Treatment of the Jewish-Arab Conflict over the land of Israel/Palestine in Israeli Textbooks' in Palestine-Israel Journal of Politics, Economic and Culture vol V No 2 p37

13 ibid p40

14 Weizman, Eyal. 2007. Hollow Land: Israel's architecture of occupation. Verso, London

15 Oz, Amos. 1983. In the Land of Israel. Fontana, London p 238

16 Sand, Shlomo. 2009. The Invention of the Jewish. People Verso, London

17 Sand, Shlomo. 2012 The Invention of the Land of Israel: From Holy Land to Homeland. Verso, London

18 Arendt, Hannah. 2006 Eichmann in Jerusalem: a report on the banality of evil. Penguin Books, London

19 Finkelstein, Norman. 2003. The Holocaust Industry: Reflections on the Exploitation of Jewish Suffering. Verso London

20 Hoffman, Eva. 2004 op cit p250

21 ibid p251

22 Hass, Amira. 2011. 'Israel-Palestine- Fear of the Future ' You Tube Sept 30th

23 Bauman, Zygmunt. 1989 .Modernity and the Holocaust. Polity Press, Cambridge.

24 ibid p 111

25 Bauman, Janina. 1987. Winter in the Morning: A Young Girl's life in the Warsaw Ghetto and Beyond. Virago Books, London

26 Bauman, Janina. 1988. A Dream of Belonging: My Years in Postwar Poland. Virago, London

27 ibid p 177

28 Hoffman, Eva 2004   op cit p255

29 Ju'beh, Nazmi. 1998 .in Dayan, Yael op cit p29

30 Khalili , Laleh. 2004. 'Grass-Roots Commemorations: Remembering the Land in the Camps of Lebanon' in Journal of Palestinian Studies vol XXXXIV No 1 p 6-22

31 Khalili, Laleh 2004 op cit p 16

32 Shehadeh, Raja. 2003. When the Bulbul Stopped Singing: A diary of Ramallah under siege. Profile Books, London p3

33 Judt, Tony 2012 (with Timothy Snyder), op cit

34 Hoffman, Eva. 1997. Shtetl: The history of a small town and an extinguished world. Secker and Warburg, London p 105

Chapter 4

1   https://archive.org/stream/EuCongratulatesIsraelOn60thAnniversary/EuCongratulatesIsraelOn60thAnniversary_djvu.txt

2   President Obama's speech in Israel 2013 http://www.whitehouse.gov/the-press-office/2013/03/21/remarks-president-barack-obama-people-israel

3   Greer Fay 'President Rivlin: Time to admit that Israel is a sick society that needs treatment' Jerusalem Post Oct 19th 2014

4   Sand, Shlomo. 'I wish to resign and cease considering myself a Jew' The Guardian Oct 10th 2014. See also his book, How I Stopped Being a Jew .Verso Books, London 2014

5   The Telegraph, October 21st 2014

6   Lally Weymouth 'An interview with Israeli Defense Minister Moshe Yaalon' The Washington Post October 24th 2014

7   The Reut Institute. 2010. Delegitimization of Israel: Creating a Political Firewall.

8   Pappe, Ilan. 2013. The Forgotten Palestinians: A history of the Palestinians in Israel. Yale University Press, New Haven and London

9   Paul Harris 'Secrets of the billionaire bankrolling Gingrich's shot at the White House" The Observer, January 29th 2012

10 Robert Mendick 'Inside the Secret Web of Tony Blair Inc' The Sunday Telegraph Jan 8th 2012

11 Pappe, Ilan. 2010. Out of the Frame; The Struggle for academic Freedom in Israel. Pluto Press, London

12 Peled-Elhanan, Nurit. 2012. Palestine in Israeli School Books: Ideology and Propaganda in Education, IB Taurus, London

13 Harriet Sherwood 'Academic Claims Israeli school textbooks contain bias' The Observer, August 7th 2011

14 ibid

15 ibid

16 Haaretz, January 27th 2012

17 Zenatti, Valérie. 2005. When I was a soldier; One girl's real story. Bloomsbury, London 2005

18 Breaking the Silence. 2012. Our Harsh Logic: Israeli Soldiers' Testimonies from the Occupied Territories, 2000-2010 . Metropolitan Books, New York

19 Ilan Pappe op cit 2010 p48

20 Blumenthal, Max. 2013, Goliath: Life and Loathing in Greater Israel. Nation Books, New York 2013 p13

21 op cit p 283

22 Friedman, Seth and Josh Friedman-Barthoud, Josh. 2010. Forty Years in the Wilderness. Five Leaves, New York

23 Jonathan Cook, 'Israel's model of political despair in Jerusalem' www.countercurrents.org Nov 26th 2014

24 The Israeli democracy Institute: http://www.en.idi.org.il

25 Cohen, Stan. 2000. States of Denial: Knowing about Atrocities and Suffering. Polity London

26 Tamar Herman and David Newman 'Israel's democratic veneer,' Jerusalem Post June 3rd 2011

27 www. Global firepower.com

27 Israel Among Leading Arms Exporters Aug 5th 2012 www. aviatinweekly.com

Chapter 5

1   Abunimah, Ali. 2014. The Battle for Justice in Palestine. Haymarket Books, London 2014

2   Robert Wade 'Organised Hypocrisy on a Monumental Scale' London Review of Books October 24th 2014

3   See Final Report: Damage Assessment and Needs Identification in the Gaza Strip published by Europe Aid with the support of the European Commission 2014 page 54

4   See http://www.addameer.org. See also the book by Abeer Baker and Anat Matar. 2011. Threat: The Palestinian political prisoners in Israel. Pluto Press, London

5   Cohen, Stan 2000. States of Denial: Knowing about Atrocities and Suffering. Polity, London 2000

6   Reports from the web-based, Palestine Chronicle

7   Human Rights Watch, World Report 2014 p558

8   http://www.epalestine.com February 5th 2012

9   Edward W. Said, 2001 Reflections on Exile: And other literary and Cultural Essays. Granta, London

10 Hilal, Jamil. 2006. 'Emigration, Conservatism and Class Formation in West Bank and Gaza Strip Communities' in L Taraki, (Ed) Living Palestine: Family Survival, Resistance and Mobility under Occupation. Syracuse University Press, New York

11 Barghouti, Mourid. 2003. I Saw Ramallah. Anchor Books, London

12 See Ana Carbajosa 2011 'Gazan youth issue manifesto to vent their anger with all sides in the conflict' The Observer January 2nd.

13 Palestinian Youth Movement http://www/www.pal-youth.org
14 Tripp, Charles. 2013. The Power of the People: paths of resistance and the Middle East. Cambridge university Press, Cambridge.
15 Mona El Farar, 2011 'International Women's Day' http://fromgaza.blogspot.com
16 Linah Alsafin, 2011 http://electronicintifada.net/blog/linah-alsaafin/israeli-soldier-cares-my-safety
17 Baramki, Gabi. 2010. Peaceful Resistance: Building a University under Occupation. Pluto Press, London

Chapter 6

1 Special Session of the Russell Tribunal on Palestine. Brussels. September 2014 para 26 (www.russeltribunalon palestine.com)
2 See 'Put Palestinians on a Diet' Information Clearing House Mov 17th 2010 (www.informationclearinghouse.info)
3 Medical Aid for Palestine (www.map-uk.org)
4 Rheinhard, Tania. 2006. The Roadmap to Nowhere`; Israel/Palestine since 2003. Verso, London
5 Adi Ophir 'Reflections on Gaza from Tel Aviv' Znet Jan 8th 2009 (zcomm.org/znetarticle/reflections-on-gaza-from-tel-aviv-by-adi-ophir/)
6 Russell Tribunal op cit
7 Alareer, Refat (Ed). 2013. Gaza Writes Back: Short stories from young writers in Gaza, Palestine. Just World Books, Virginia p 25
8 op cit p 22
9 op cit p22
10 op cit p24
11 The Goldstone Report 2009 United Nations Human Rights Council Report on the Gaza Conflict
12 The Palestinian Trauma Centre 'Psychological Support for Gaza.' International Solidarity Movement April 30th 2014 (www.palsolidarity.org)

13   Palestinian Centre for Human Rights 2013 'Through Women's Eyes"
     Gender-specific report on the latest Israeli offensive' (http://www.
     pchrgaza.org)

14   op cit p 42

15   Mai Yaghi 2014 'Gaza children left orphaned by bloody war' http://
     news.yahoo.com/gaza-children-left-orphaned-bloody-war-223052646.
     html August 28. See also Yaghi, Rawan. 2013. 'From Beneath' in Gaza
     Writes Back: Short stories from young writers in Gaza, Palestine. Just
     World Books. op cit

16   2010See more at: http://justworldbooks.com/from-beneath-a-gaza-
     childs-story-by-rawan-yaghi/#sthash.TOUE9IlA.dpuf

17   Levy, Gideon. 2010. The Punishment of Gaza. Verso, London

Chapter 7

1   Daniel Barenboim, 2014 'Germany Must talk straight with Israel' The
     Guardian Nov 10th

2   Gideon Levy, 2013 'Time to be simple-minded' Haaretz, April 28th

3   ibid

4   Peace Direct, http://www.peacedirect.org

5   The Peres Centre, http://www.peres.centre.org

6   Coalition of Women for Peace http://www.whoprofits.org

7   Combatant for Peace http://cfperace.org

8   Breaking the Silence http://www.peacedirect.org

9   Refuser Solidarity Network http://www.refusersolidarity.net

10   Jewish Voice for Peace http://jewishvoiceforpeace.org

11   European Jews for a Just Peace http://www.ejjp.org

12   The Shit List http://www.masada2000.org/shit-list.html

13   (quoted by Asa Winstanley in Inform, Jan 3rd 2012. See also www.
     winstanleys.org

14   Lord Jonathan Sacks, 2014. 'Europe's Alarming New Anti-Semitism',
     Wall Street Journal Oct.

15 For the key document of the Boycott Disinvestment and Sanction
    (BDS). See Omar Barghouti, 2011. BDS: The global struggle for
    Palestinian rights. Hamarket Books, Chicago
16 Speech to the Knesset, March 2014 https://www.gov.uk/government/
    speeches/david-camerons-speech-to-the-knesset-in-israel)
17 See http://www.theguardian.com/global-development/
    interactive/2011/oct/05/dfid-future-aid-plans-interactive
18 Andreas Hackl. 2014 'Analysis of EU aid to Palestine – help or
    hindrance?' In Irin, Jan www.irinnews.org
19 Natalie Tocci 'The EU, the Middle East Quartet and (in)effective
    multilaterialism' Mercury Papers www.iai.it
20 Ora Coren and Nada Feldman, 2013 'US aid to Israel totals $233.7
    billion over six decades 'www. Haaretz. Com March 20th
21 (http://www.ustr.gov/countries-regions/europe-middle-east/middle-
    east/north-africa/israel)
22 Howard Eisenstadt .2012 'Wait, Whose the super power here? Slate
    Sept 20th www.slate.com

Chapter 8

1   Ali Abunimah http://electronicintifada.net/blogs/ali-abunimah/why-i-
    want-obama-veto-abbas-un-resolution-palestine
2   Richard Falk, 2014 ' The Dead End of Post-Oslo Diplomacy: What
    next?' http://www.foreignpolicyjournal.com/2014/12/18/
3   Tony Judt, 2003 'Israel: The Alternative' New York Review of Books Oct
    23rd. 2
4   Judt, Tony (with Timothy Snyder). 2012. Thinking the Twentieth
    Century. William Heinemann, London page 125
5   Sam Bahour   © bitterlemons.org 23/1/2012
6   Cronin, David. 2012. 'The Rise of the Israel Lobby in Europe' in Daud
    Abdullah and Ibrahim Hewitt (Eds) In the Battle for Public Opinion
    in Europe: Changing Perception of the Palestine-Israel Conflict .Memo
    Publishers, London

7 Philo, Greg and Berry, M. 2011. More Bad News from Israel. Pluto books, London

8 Tim Llewellyn, 2012 'A Public Ignored: The Broadcasters' False Portrayal of the Israel-Palestine Struggle ' in Daud Abdullah and Ibrahim Hewitt op cit

9 Tim Llewellyn op cit p35

10 Said, Edward. 1978. Orientalism. Random House, New York

11 Jonathon Tobin, 'Care about the Jewish state's future? Obama in an interview reveals even more reasons to worry http://www.jewishworldreview.com/0814/tobin081114. php3#qSgqG2HS6Emi6B0t.99

12 An Open Letter to American Jews in http://www. Israelisforasustainablefuture.com, August 2014

13 Independent Jewish Voices www.ijv.org.uk

14 http://electronicintifada.net/blogs/adri-nieuwhof/israel-has-no-right-be-apartheid-state-says-boycott-within-founder

15 Ofra Yeshua-Lyth and the case for a new Israel in Arpan Roy http://mondoweiss.net/2014/10/ofra-yeshua-israeli#sthash.wz4ONE6G.dpuf October 9, 2014

16 See: http://mondoweiss.net/2014/10/ofra-yeshua-israeli#sthash.wz4ONE6G.dpuf

17 See the 'One Democratic State conference 'in Zurich, ODS Zurich Conference May 2014 Q&A Ghada Karmi and Ilan Pappe https://www.youtube.com/watch?v=YjmDujYubuo

18 Levine, Mark and Mossberg Mathias. 2014 .One Land, Two States: Israel and Palestine as parallel states. University of California Press. See also http://tabletmag.com/jewish-news-and-politics/181181/mossberg-parallel-states

19 Halpern, G. 2008/ An Israeli in Palestine: Resisting Dispossession, Redeeming Israel. Pluto Press, London p 208

Chapter 9

1   For an account of the BDS movement se: Omar Barghouti, 2011.
    Boycott Disinvestment and Sanctions: The global struggle for
    Palestinians rights. Haymarket Books, Chicago

2   Time for Action: A British Christian response to A Moment of Truth,
    the Kairos Palestine Document. www.kairosbritain.org.uk 2013

3   Rachel Corrie was a member of the International Solidarity Movement
    killed in Rafah in Gaza in 2003 trying to protect a Palestinian home
    from being bulldozed. The Rachel Corrie foundation exists to promote
    principles of peace and human rights across the world. http://
    rachelcorriefoundation.org

4   Mondweiss.net is a website publishing materials about the Middle East
    from a liberal Jewish perspective that are critical of American Foreign
    Policy. See http://mondoweiss.net The electronic intifada is a web
    based campaign, news and blogging to promote Palestinian human
    rights. Its co-founder and Director is, Ali Abunimah author of The
    Battle for Palestine, Haymarket Books, Chicago 2014 See http://
    electronicintifada.net

5   General assembly of the United Nations, The Question of Palestine
    http://unispal.un.org/unispal.nsf/iss.htm?OpenForm

6   See Cronin, David. 2011. Europe's Alliance with Israel: Aiding the
    occupation, Pluto Press, London

7   World Bank Press Release October 30th 2014: World Bank Endorses
    New Strategy for Palestinian Territories and Approves US$62 million
    for Reconstruction in Gaza . See also Gaza: Accelerating Recovery
    September 12th 2014 http://www.worldbank.org

8   See Brookings Institute, Shibley Telhami, 'American Public Attitudes
    Towards the Israel-Palestine Conflict.' December 5th 2014 http://www.
    brookings.edu
    The Economist 2015, 'Us and them' August 2nd 2015. See also the
    world public opinion surveys. In 2013 this showed Israel to have a
    negative public image in the majority of countries surveyed. http://
    www.worldpublicopinion.org

9   Kepel, Gilles, 2004. The War for Muslim Minds: Islam and the West, Harvard University Press, Cambridge Mass.

10   Fisk, Robert. 2006. The Great War for Civilization: The conquest of the Middle East. Harper Collins, London page 557

11   ibid p 558

12   Oz, Amos. 2002. 'Between right and right ' in How to Cure a Fanatic, Princeton University Press, Princeton

13   ibid p 35

14   Mason, Paul 2013 Why It's Still Kicking Off Everywhere: The new global revolutions, Verso, London

Index

Two more books in the Radical Read Series

The Cost of Living Crisis
by Michael Calderbank

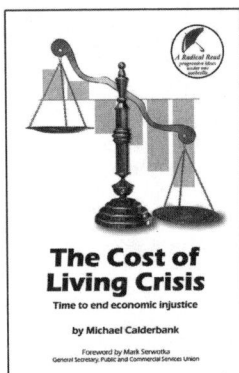

In this book the author delivers an uncompromising message to the political elite: the politics of austerity is an act of economic injustice that must be corrected.

"An invaluable weapon in the hands of all those refuting and rejecting austerity."

John McDonnell, Shadow Chancellor

The Failed Experiment
by Andrew Fisher

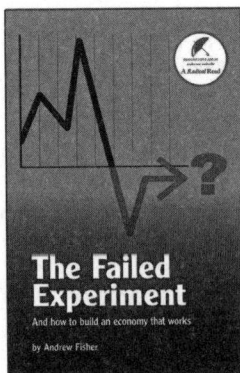

It is politicians not bankers that must take most of the blame for 2008 financial collapse. This is a book about the much larger political crisis that still threatens our living standards - and how we can resolve it.

"Will be used by campaigners as a basic handbook to explain our recent history."

John McDonnell, Shadow Chancellor

Due to be launched for the Labour Party 2016 Conference

Two new stimulating books in the Radical Read series

From Hardie to Corbyn
What ever happened to the Labour Party?

Since the Labour Party's foundation, effective power has rested with a small élite: the Leader, the Parliamentary Labour Party and those who head the major trade unions. The outcome has been a pragmatic programme and three major periods of election success. There have been achievements, but none significant enough to make Labour the natural party of power.

On a few occasions the collective voice of the membership has determined policy. The election of Jeremy Corbyn looks like being one of them.

For those who want to understand if the Labour Party has a future, this challenging historic analysis is an essential read.

A Turn to the Left
Making radical policies electable

Politicians are either weathervanes or signposts.

To be a signpost is difficult, but it is the only way radical change in society can be made. The Labour Party has secured its most worthwhile achievements when it has moved to the left.

Michael Calderbank, joint editor of Red Pepper, issued a challenge to experts in fields as diverse as National Defence and the Media. He invited them to explain how radical solutions can be presented in a way that is acceptable to the electorate. The outcome is a realistic strategy that needs to make no compromises in the struggle to achieve a fair and just society.

Receive the latest information about Radical Read publications.
Subscribe at www.radicalread.co.uk or email us at info@radicalread.co.uk.